THE FOUR HORSEMEN OF DENTISTRY

Survival Strategies for the Private Dental Practice Under Siege

COLIN RECEVEUR

CEO
SmartBox

Copyright © 2017 by Colin Receveur. All rights reserved.

No part of this publication may be reproduced, stored in a retrieval system, or transmitted by any means electronic, mechanical, photocopying, recording, or otherwise, without prior written permission from SmartBox, LLC. Published & printed in the United States of America. Any person flouting the above rules will be liable for copyright infringement.

For permissions or more information, please write to:

821 Mount Tabor Road, Suite 300, New Albany, IN 47150
Toll Free: 888.741.1413 - **Fax:** 502.371.0659

ISBN: 978-0-692-89278-7

colin@smartboxwebmarketing.com
www.smartboxwebmarketing.com

Facebook: www.fb.me/SmartBoxWebMarketing
Twitter: @creceveur
YouTube: www.youtube.com/SmartBoxWeb

To my loving wife, Manja, who has abided my moods, supported my whims, been my biggest cheerleader, and given us three terrific kids.

Contents

Foreword		IX
Introduction		XI
Chapter 1	It's a (Corporate) Jungle Out There	1
Chapter 2	"Kids" These Days	9
Chapter 3	The Squeeze Is On	19
Chapter 4	When Things Go Smash ... Again	25
Chapter 5	The Patient Attraction System™	35
Chapter 6	The First Pillar: Attraction	67
Chapter 7	The Second Pillar: Conversion	93
Chapter 8	The Third Pillar: Follow-Up	123
Chapter 9	The Fourth Pillar: Tracking	143
Afterword	You Can Triumph in the Coming War	161
Appendix	Additional Patient Attraction Resources	183

"I can say with all confidence that Colin Receveur knows what he's doing to leverage the internet to help dentists attract more and better patients."

— Dr. Michael Abernathy
FOUNDER, SUMMIT PRACTICE SOLUTIONS

"I've been a client of Colin Receveur since 2013. I already had a prominent web presence. Colin and his brilliant team were quickly able to consolidate and automate our online programs – email responses, phone tracking and recording, press releases, blog posts, Infusionsoft integration with ortho and implant campaign sequences."

— Dr. Mitchel Friedman
LINCROFT, NEW JERSEY

"The last six months, six to eight months, have been very exceptional. I've had more new patients than I've ever had. We're doing a lot better this year than we did last year, and I was extremely happy with last year. If I had it to do over, there's absolutely no doubt I would join SmartBox."

— Dr. Thomas Feder
BELLEVILLE, ILLINOIS

"I'm not all that savvy on the internet with marketing and things like that. I just know that's not my thing. I liked what Colin had to say. We got in touch with SmartBox and felt like we needed to make that change, so we left our other marketing expert and turned to you guys, and we're happy we did."

    – Dr. Lawrence T. Fox
      BURKE, VIRGINIA

"For SmartBox, what really was interesting to me was to see that you can set it up until the person feels like you're an expert. They look at it from a holistic approach. It's not just search and optimization, it's not just pay-per-click, it's not just the website revisions, not just SEO, it's not just social media. It's the whole combination."

    – Corey Hurcomb
      TULIP TREE DENTAL CARE, SOUTH BEND, INDIANA

"The return on investment is great. SmartBox has done a great job generating phone calls, no question about that. Our new patients are up markedly from when our website went live."

    – Dr. Matthew Burton
      CLEARWATER, FLORIDA

"There are many companies out there, but they're not dental specialists, if you will, in the marketing, whereas that's what SmartBox is. It's the big picture. It's the marketing. It's putting all the different aspects together and making it a complete package for promoting my practice. Drive the patients from the website to my practice."

– Dr. Doug Forbes
SOUTH CAROLINA

Foreword

My name is Colin Receveur, and I have a clear vision of what I want to build in this world.

I imagine a world in which the vast majority of dentists wake up inspired by their profession every single morning. They enjoy providing great care for their patients, and they return home fulfilled at the end of the day. And everything I do – whether writing, speaking, teaching, or consulting – is devoted to helping build that world.

Being the son of a (now) very successful dentist, I saw firsthand the struggles my father faced in establishing and maintaining a successful business. I remember the impact that the lean months, and even a few lean years, had on the family.

I like to think that I "get" the business of dentistry better than most, in a very personal way.

In my teens, I discovered a love for the internet, back when it was first becoming something more than a curiosity. That love grew into a passion for internet marketing, and I determined that I would use my expertise and knowledge of dentistry to help dentists thrive.

I saw the flaws in how dentists traditionally advertise to get new patients. Those insights led to the development of my revolutionary, industry-leading Patient Attraction System™.

Now, I've seen something else – something alarming. That's why I wrote this book – to warn dentists about what well may be a calamity for many dental practices if they don't prepare.

Foreword

In this book, you'll find the roadmap for dentists to not only survive but also thrive during difficult times, even during a recession, no matter the forces working against them.

I'm dedicated to helping dentists succeed. I've got a soft spot for dentists, and I'm funny that way. And I know with everything in me that if dentists don't take action soon, too many of them will fail.

Your dental practice is under siege right now, whether you know it or not. Read, consider, and take action – please.

Keep Moving Forward,

Introduction

No More Sleepless Nights

I was talking with a dentist the other day whose practice is located in a city of about 40,000 people on the Eastern Seaboard. I found out quickly that things were not going well for him.

"My competition is increasing," he told me. "There have been three new dentists who opened practices in the last year within a couple miles of mine. My collections are down about 12 percent compared to last year. Last year they were down five percent. Insurance reimbursement flat sucks, although that's true for all of us. And now, I've heard that one of the chains is nosing around, too. If corporate comes into my market, I don't know what I'm going to do."

I appreciated his honesty. As CEO of SmartBox, I've talked with a lot of dentists – thousands of them, in fact. Quite a few of those dentists weren't willing to admit just how bad things had become for them.

This doctor has been in practice for about 15 years. He's beginning to reconsider his retirement plans, even though he's only about 45 years old. "I'm torn," he said. "I always thought that I'd stay in practice until I was about 60 and then go out on top. Now, I wonder whether I'm going to make it that long. And what kind of shape the practice will be in when I get there. I've thought about selling, but I owe a lot to my staff. I don't feel like I can just abandon them. I'm just worried that my downturn is going to continue. It's tough to sell a declining practice. I probably couldn't get what it's worth."

At his request, I took a deep dive into his dental marketing. It was easy to see why he was getting less than he'd gotten before. It was also clear to me that if he doesn't take a different approach to getting more new patients who aren't price shoppers, insurance-driven, or one-and-dones, his practice was in trouble.

This particular doctor didn't mention it during our phone call, but I'd guess that he's had more than a few sleepless nights trying to figure out how to save his practice.

How Do Things Look from Where You Stand?

Depending on how you're approaching your dental marketing, your outlook might be fairly rosy or pretty bleak.

If your dental practice is doing well, you should be very proud of yourself and of the people you employ. It's never easy to be a small business owner. But this is no time for complacency. As you'll learn in this book, there are storm clouds on the horizon.

If things aren't looking so good, the first thing you should consider is your marketing.

Most dentists advertise like most other dentists. Maybe you do, too. You "chase" patients through discounts, specials, and insurance acceptance. That's the traditional dental advertising approach, and the wonder is that it's held on for so many years.

Some dentists still get pretty decent results from advertising. Others, not so much. Chasing patients gets you price shoppers, one-and-dones, and insurance-driven patients. You can build a practice with those low-value cases, but you'll work extra hours and extra hard.

That's what you can do **right now**, but not for much longer.

The days of getting new patients through traditional advertising are rapidly coming to an end, and dentists need to be warned. That's why I wrote this book – to alert dentists everywhere to the coming "dental apocalypse" that is putting your livelihood at risk.

What's looming on the horizon is nothing less than a fundamental shift in how dentists will make their living. It's a game-changer unlike anything the industry has seen before, and if you're not prepared, you may very well fail.

A Convergence of Forces

There are three ongoing macroeconomic trends – the "Unholy Trinity" – that are converging to pose a major challenge to private dentists. There's a fourth "force" that has the potential to usher in the equivalent of private dentistry's last days.

The Unholy Trinity consists of the rise of corporate dentistry, increased competition due to more new dental graduates, and declining insurance reimbursements. You've undoubtedly read about each of those trends or heard them discussed at meetings.

But have you ever stopped to consider how they work together to make any dentist's life a **nightmare**? This is one of those "The whole is greater than the sum of the parts" scenarios. I'll analyze the impact of each, but the Unholy Trinity isn't your only challenge.

When you add in the specter of economic uncertainty, you have the dental equivalent of the Four Horsemen of the Apocalypse.

If that sounds like hype, think again. Never before has dentistry faced the coming together of challenges like these.

The Corporate Dentistry Conquerors

In many respects, corporate dentistry is no different than any other corporate venture. It goes where the money is, even if making that money requires putting competitors out of business.

And there's money to be made both within and outside of major metropolitan areas.

Smaller communities are feeling the effects of corporate dentistry's presence. Take a look at Aspen Dental's office listings; you'll be amazed at some of the comparatively small cities that have Aspen offices. Just to name a few not that far from SmartBox headquarters (in the greater Louisville, Kentucky, area), there are Aspen offices in Vincennes, Indiana (population 18,000 as of 2013); Georgetown, Kentucky (about 31,000 as of 2013); and Middletown, Ohio (2013 population about 49,000).

You might think that one corporate dental office isn't that bad in a smaller town. You'd be wrong.

Aspen Dental isn't everywhere in the U.S., but it's working on it. However, more regional corporate chains are well established and pose a serious threat. Check out Heartland Dental, which is heavily clustered in the eastern half of the U.S. There are smaller chains targeting California, Texas, and Florida that rarely seem to make the news – but they're out there.

If the opportunity presents and the numbers are right, corporate will move into your market – if it's not already there. That's not good news for private dental practices for several reasons.

A Shot to the Trust

Corporate dentistry is bad news for private dental practices and for the industry as a whole. As the host of lawsuits suggests, corporate dentists are under tremendous pressure to produce results, measured by collections. That has led to recommending and providing unnecessary treatment, poorly performed dentistry, and repeated billing "errors."

In June 2015, the New York Attorney General announced the settlement of a suit against Aspen Dental that required the company to pay a penalty of nearly half a million dollars. The settlement also ensured that Aspen would not be involved with clinical decisions within its practices. Aspen agreed not to split patients' fees with the clinics. Finally, consumers will be informed that the management company is not a dental service provider.

The dental industry has worked long and hard to build patients' trust, and a few bad actors can diminish those gains. Let me say here that there are certainly corporate dental offices that provide appropriate, reasonable quality work. I can't be sure whether those corporate practices are in the majority or the minority. But the offices that are operating ethically are doing so *in spite* of pressures from above.

Corporate dentistry has the potential to give dentists everywhere a bad name.

Racing to the Bottom

Beyond the issue of trust, corporate dentistry has the effect of driving down prices for dental work. Low-price dentistry is a challenge for dentists who don't enjoy the economies of scale that corporate offices realize. If your competitors are offering the same procedure for 25 percent less than you can manage, that resets your prospects' expectations of a "reasonable" charge. Independent dentists' margins are getting squeezed, and that trend will continue.

Corporate dentistry also has deeper advertising and marketing "pockets" than almost all private dentists. Individual practices can go broke trying to match the typical corporate advertising blitz. Too many dental prospects think first of a well-known corporate dental office because that's what they've seen the most often. Corporate dentistry siphons away your prospects.

Corporate dentistry also squeezes your practice due to its wider appointment availability. Extended weekday and weekend hours are the norm, which fits many patients' schedules better.

That Sinking Feeling

Corporate dentistry is bad news for private dentists. Whether you know it or not, they've got you in their crosshairs – today, tomorrow, or next year. The logical extension of corporate's operating philosophy is to eliminate competitors – like you – and consolidate a market's dental service provision under its umbrella.

If you're still chasing patients through traditional advertising, be warned: corporate dentistry can afford to "besiege" your practice until you have no choice but to run up the white flag.

That's why corporate dentistry is **the First Horseman – Conquest.**

The doctor I was talking with knows this, and it scares him.

A Plague of New Dental Graduates

After a long dry spell of no growth, dental schools began sprouting up again after the turn of the century. As of this writing, there are more than 65 dental schools in the U.S. and more are planned. Those dental schools are expected to graduate **between 5,500 and 6,000 new dentists** *every year.*

At the same time, the costs of dental school have ballooned to the point where the average debt load for graduates is sending them straight into the arms of corporate dentistry so they can begin paying those debts. New dentists are fuel for the corporate machine until they're able to arrange financing to establish their own practice or acquire an existing one.

While they're employed by corporate chains, they'll be subject to the pressures I mentioned earlier – to produce by recommending unnecessary procedures and using inferior materials. As new graduates with overwhelming debt and few alternatives, many of them will comply. After all, they really **need** those jobs. That can only further erode the trust that is the essence of the doctor-patient relationship.

Spinning Off

Once those new graduates leave corporate dentistry – with little or no debt, and possibly with considerable savings – they'll present another kind of threat. They'll be positioned to have successful private practices, either by opening their own offices or purchasing existing practices from retiring dentists.

It's a double-edged sword. New graduates continually fuel the corporate dentistry machine and eventually emerge as new, individual competitors. Dental schools keep churning out new graduates who refuel the corporate machine.

And those new dentists are **used** to this connected online world, probably more so than you. They won't think twice about embracing online advertising in a big way. As you'll see later, that's where most of your new prospects look for you these days. You'll have to level that playing field, if you haven't done so already.

With a plague of competition for a limited dental prospect pool, each dentist's share will get smaller and smaller.

That's why new dental school graduates are **the Second Horseman – Pestilence.**

The Slow Starvation of Insurance Reimbursements

Declining insurance reimbursements are squeezing dentists everywhere, and there's no end in sight to the trend.

The gap between the cost of providing a service and reimbursement for that service has widened over the years. Some people believe that all dental insurance reimbursement is headed toward PPO rates. Dentists may not be able to use optimal materials for restorations because they simply won't get paid for the additional cost.

With less insurance money coming in, the burden of payment is shifted more to patients, who may decline procedures due to out-of-pocket costs. That means less money coming from both sources.

Dentists who rely on insurance reimbursements will find their practices starving for cash. That's why reimbursements are **the Third Horseman – Famine.**

On a Pale Horse?

You've already seen that the Unholy Trinity will pose major challenges to the survival of your dental practice. But the effects of those three forces – corporate dentistry, new dental graduates, and declining reimbursements – are intensified in the presence of an uncertain economic outlook.

If the last seven years have proven anything, it's that a seemingly strong economy can suffer a major recession at almost any time. As of this writing, a new Administration is trying to find its feet. But that hasn't stopped them from beginning to dismantle a number of initiatives that, while either loved and despised, have lent a certain security to the U.S. economy.

That certainty is rapidly evaporating, and dentists will feel the effects as patients defer needed care to hoard their funds against the possibility of job loss. That will be a direct hit to your bottom line, but it's nothing compared to the pain you'll feel when everything goes *smash*.

Would Your Dental Practice Survive?

You have commitments to your family, to your staff, and to your patients. In the face of another recession, you'll have less money coming in, meaning you'll struggle to honor those commitments. If you've thought about what you'd do if the economy tanked, I wouldn't be surprised if you've had more than a few sleepless nights wondering how you're going to turn things around. You might even have wondered a time or two whether you'd be able to keep the doors open.

Economic uncertainty is **the Fourth Horseman – Death.**

It Could Happen To You

Dr. P is a dentist in the Midwest who's been in practice for about three years.

"Sometimes, I question my decision to buy this practice," he told me. "It looked like a good deal, but things haven't gone the way I expected them to."

Dr. P did everything he should have before buying that practice from a retiring dentist. His due diligence was flawless. What he couldn't have anticipated the sudden closure of a major employer in his market.

"It's like a wasteland around here," he said. "Maybe a third of the community was employed by a manufacturing firm. That company had been in business for at least 50 years. I checked, and it looked solid. But the same year I bought my practice, the factory was acquired by a conglomerate. I hadn't heard a word that anything like that was in the works. And within a year, the plant was shuttered. All of a sudden, nobody has dental insurance. My chairs are empty at least 20 percent of the time, and it's taking a toll. I've had to discount heavily to keep people coming in, but it's still not enough. I've asked around, and my competitors – we're pretty friendly, here – are in the same boat."

He paused for a moment and mopped his face. Finally, he said, "The only question is which practice will close up shop first."

Do You Hear Hoofbeats?

I haven't painted a pretty picture for the future of your dental practice. You don't need pretty pictures. You need a clear, cold-eyed, objective look at what you're facing.

Now, things may not be going badly for you at the moment. But since you're reading this book, I have to assume that you're looking for something better than what you have right now. Or you've already wondered whether your current smooth sailing is going to last.

If you've had sleepless nights, I'm quite certain that you're more than willing to avoid those in the future.

I'm a small business owner, and I know exactly how it feels at three o'clock in the morning and you have way more questions than answers. I have the answers to most dentists' 3 a.m. self-doubt. Notice that I said "most." That's because the information in this book will turn what you believe about dental marketing on its head.

Not all dentists are willing to make the mental shift required to embrace a new way of doing things. Others simply aren't in a financial position to capitalize on a proven system of attracting more and better dental patients.

The Four Horsemen of Dentistry – corporate dentistry, new dental graduates, declining reimbursements, and economic uncertainty – are coming for your dental practice, and you had better be ready.

Most dentists are not.

I'm going to take a deeper dive into the challenges facing dentists these days before laying out a **proven** system that may be the solution to your problems. Before I do, let me ask you a couple things:

Is your current dental marketing bringing a return on investment between **1700 and 4600 percent?**

If not, do you know why? I'll show you later in this book. I'll also show you how you can enjoy the position of strength that comes with attracting not only **more** new patients but **better** new patients.

Is your marketing attracting the cases you **love** to handle? Or are you largely getting a bunch of drill-and-fills, one-offs, and insurance-driven patients?

If it's the latter, you've definitely bought the right book. You won't survive what's coming without knowing how to combat the forces coming for your practice.

In the following chapters, I'll take a deeper dive into each of the Four Horsemen. Sun Tzu, who wrote *The Art of War*, tells you why that's necessary:

> **If you know the enemy and know yourself, you need not fear the result of a hundred battles. If you know yourself but not the enemy, for every victory gained you will also suffer a defeat. If you know neither the enemy nor yourself, you will succumb in every battle.**

If you're going to successfully battle the Four Horsemen of Dentistry, you need to know your enemies. Let's get started.

Not-So-Fun Fact:

Consumer spending on dentistry has basically been flat since 2008.

1
It's a (Corporate) Jungle Out There

> "Never fight fair with a stranger, boy.
> You'll never get out of the jungle that way."
> - Arthur Miller, *Death of a Salesman*

Today's dentistry is a jungle, and it's survival of the fittest. When it comes to you versus corporate dentistry, it's not anything like a fair fight. You might be a lion among dentists, but even a lion can be taken down by a pack of jackals.

Did you know that jackals are omnivorous? They eat everything and anything.

That sounds a lot like corporate dentistry.

Really Low-Hanging Fruit

In a 2015 study by CareCredit, slightly more than two-thirds of dental patients showed themselves to be cost-conscious health care consumers. Those patients researched procedure costs and inquired about financing.

Assuming this trend holds, and there's no reason to think that it won't, **two out of three** of your prospects are cost-driven.

That's exactly the segment corporate dentistry targets with much of its advertising. That's an advertising presence you'll struggle to match. As you've already read, corporate dentistry has deeper pockets than almost any private practice, and here's why.

It's a Question of Scale

Corporate dentistry enjoys enormous economies of scale that a single practitioner or even a small group practice can't hope to match.

1. **Administration:** Centralizing support services reduces overhead. Instead of each practice needing a bookkeeper, Human Resources asset, and an office manager, several practices or more are serviced by just a few people.

2. **Purchasing:** Corporate dentistry can purchase supplies, materials, and equipment in larger quantities at lower rates. In some instances, corporate can even purchase retiring dentists' practices at a lower cost than a single practitioner could negotiate.

3. **Negotiating:** The largest corporate dental chains can negotiate higher reimbursement rates from managed care organizations. That's more money in their pockets, and a stronger market position, than you can manage.

4. **Availability:** By one estimate, most corporate practices operate on a 50- to 60-hour workweek compared to the common 32-hour workweek of private dental practices. The same location can generate a great deal more revenue without incurring comparable overhead.

5. **Staffing:** With corporate's extended hours, they're in a good position to rotate just enough ancillary personnel to cover a shift's needs rather than staffing up to handle all situations. Just as important, specialists can rotate between offices, decreasing the need to establish a specialist in each practice.

6. **Pricing:** The first five points drive the last one – pricing. Corporate dentistry has much deeper pockets than you do, can generate significantly more revenue, and can save more on

operational costs. Corporate will eat you alive if you try to go head-to-head against them on cost per procedure. Competing on price is a race to the bottom that you can't hope to win.

But as you've seen, that's what drives at least two-thirds of dental patients – the cost of dental care. If corporate can dominate that cost-conscious segment in a given market, it leaves the other dentists, including you, battling it out for a greatly reduced pool of dental patients.

Not only will corporate outcompete you on price, but they'll also drive down the going rate for procedures in your area. The CEO of one regional dental chain boasts that its practice overhead in New Mexico is 45 percent instead of the 70 percent that is more typical for the independent practice. With that kind of margin, corporate offices can easily undercut your prices for longer than you can afford.

You may already have found yourself discounting your usual rates just to keep a patient who found a better "deal" at a corporate office. If you haven't had to do that, just wait.

Yes, They're Coming

If you think corporate wouldn't be interested in your market, you're wrong.

Roughly 4 out of 10 of dentists are baby boomers or older. That's a lot of retiring dentists coming up and a lot of dental practices for sale. One or more of those practices could very well be in your market.

Some retiring dentists refuse to sell to corporate dentistry. The other most likely purchasers are newly debt-free dentists who are done working for corporate practices. In some ways, that's an improvement compared to trying to compete against a corporate dental practice. But it's still competition, and as I've mentioned, if corporate isn't in your area yet, it will be.

In fact, corporate dentistry doesn't even have to be in your market to damage your practice. A corporate chain in the next market over can siphon off significant numbers of your dental prospects. Most people will make a 40- or 50-mile round trip to save a few hundred bucks. The patients on the edge of your market will desert, and the odds are you won't get them back.

Fuel for the Corporate Fire

According to the American Dental Education Association, the debt burden on new dental graduates (an average of over $260,000 for the class of 2016, and more than $300,000 for 30 percent) is extremely high.

That enormous debt level is a disincentive for many new graduates to immediately open their own practices. Heavily indebted graduates are fuel for the corporate dentistry fire.

According to salary.com, the median salary for a U.S. dentist is $146,154. Most newly graduated dentists can go to work for a corporate office with a realistic salary expectation of around $120,000 to $130,000 (higher in some areas) while paying nothing for business operations. That's a lot of discretionary income to pay down school debt. In the worst-case scenario – $300,000 in school debt – a dentist could easily bring that balance to zero in as little as five years.

What's even more interesting is that about 20 percent of new graduates have zero to less than $100,000 in debt. With the salary range just mentioned, it would take around 18 months to be debt-free. Those newly minted dentists are in an excellent position to open their own practices now, or after a fairly short stint with a corporate chain to pay down or pay off their debt.

Not all new, heavily indebted graduates choose corporate dentistry. Some are joining larger, non-chain dental practices. At some point, many of those new graduates will feel comfortable enough with their financial situation to explore opening their own practices or acquiring existing practices. And they – and you – will be competing for that reduced pool of dental prospects.

But it won't be all individual dental practices that are competing head-to-head – some knowledgeable industry wonks predict that non-corporate group practices will become more and more common in the near future. And while those group practices may not have all the economies of scale that the larger chains have, they have more than you.

This isn't just speculation. *JADA* noted in 2014 that the trend toward larger, consolidated dental practices is going to continue.

If this goes on, **and it will**, how will you compete?

Corporate is coming, and it has the potential to eat your dental practice alive if you try to compete on its terms.

No one is predicting an end to corporate dentistry's growing influence and power. In fact, one prediction is that by 2018, corporate dentistry will employ *one dentist in six!*

Corporate dentistry is all about Conquest, and it's aiming at you.

I've been steadily warning dentists about the rise of the corporate machine for some years now. And that was before this perfect storm of forces came together to create the extremely challenging situation that dentists face today.

It Happened to Him

I was talking with Dr. D. the other day. He's a well-established dentist who practices in a larger city in the South. Given the size of the market, I was somewhat surprised when he said corporate dentistry had taken a toll on his income. I asked him for specifics.

"A corporate chain got here about two years ago," he told me. "We're a in a pretty good-sized market, so I wasn't anticipating a lot of problems. I was wrong. They've got billboards all over town. They've got TV commercials and radio spots running constantly. There's maybe two or three dentists in this area who have the budget to even try to match that. I'm not one of them."

"Anything else?" I asked.

"I've taken a hit online," he replied. "Those corporate shops are all over the first page of local search results on Google. Not just their listings, but that's bad enough. My own listing has gotten bumped to the second page of results, and I'm feeling it. Our new patient numbers are down. And the chain has paid ads on Google with heavily discounted prices. Anybody who looks for a dentist online in this area can't help but see them."

"But you're still keeping your existing patients?" I asked.

"Most of them," he said. "I really thought my patients appreciated quality dental care. Turns out that a lot of the patients I thought were loyal are looking for a better deal on price."

What's in Your Arsenal?

If yours is a one- or two-dentist practice, you've got some big guns arrayed against you. Basically, the corporate chains have modern automatic weapons. You, with your traditional approach to dental marketing, have six-shooters.

The smart money favors the force with the biggest guns. The odds, as they say, are not in your favor.

There is a way to change the balance of power, and that's to find a secret weapon that corporate can't hope to match. Such a weapon exists, and it's been proven effective in many hundreds of field trials. If this secret weapon didn't function as advertised, there'd be no reason to write this book. I'd be just another "alarmist" trying to make a buck. Instead, I'm giving you the means not only to fight off corporate dentistry but to take the high ground.

Here's a hint, again from Sun Tzu:

To secure ourselves against defeat lies in our own hands, but the opportunity of defeating the enemy is provided by the enemy himself.

Since corporate dentistry is only one of the Four Horsemen of Dentistry, let's move on. You have to know all your enemies' weaknesses before you can draw up an effective battle plan.

Not-So-Fun Fact:

According to Wells Fargo, many dental management organizations expect an annual growth rate of 20 percent. They're looking to double the number of locations over the next three years.

2
"Kids" These Days

I was talking with an older, established dentist who told me that a couple of new dental grads had opened a joint practice not far from his.

"I thought I'd check them out," he told me, "so I went online and looked up their website. I couldn't believe what I was seeing! The way it was laid out, how the information just kind of naturally flowed and led patients along ... it was a work of art, I'm telling you. I finished looking it over, shook my head, and said, 'Damn!' And then I brought up my old website – I don't think we've touched it for five years – and I shook my head, and said, "Damn."

The "kids" are coming, and you'd better be ready.

Demand and Supply

There were about 5,500 Dental Health Professional Shortage Areas in the U.S. as of early 2017, according to the federal government. That's a lot of underserved dental patients who will require a lot of new dentists. Around 8.100 new dentists, in fact, according to the Health Resources and Services Administration.

With demand comes supply, and dental schools are taking note. After a wave of closures leading up to the year 2000, dental schools are enjoying a resurgence. At present, there are more than 65 dental schools in the United States with several more slated to open within a few years.

Those schools graduated around 6,000 new dentists in 2016, according to the ADA Health Policy Institute. Not all of those dentists will pursue their careers in underserved areas. Many of them will establish new practices in markets very much like yours.

But these aren't your typical dentists.

Dentists with a Difference

If you're not that long out of dental school yourself, you probably share the traits I'm going to discuss. On the other hand, if you've been in practice for a decade or more, the memories of what it's like to be young and newly turned loose on the world may have dimmed a bit.

Either way, new dental graduates are a force to be reckoned with, because they have a drive and a hunger that are equally inspiring and terrifying. By one estimate, more than three-fourths of the world's workers will belong to the same generation as these new dentists by 2025 – millennials.

The most recent crop of dental graduates, generally in their mid- to late-20s, are millennials, or the so-called "Generation Y." The exact generational boundary years differ, but for the purposes of this discussion let's consider that these people were born between 1977 and 1995. That means that roughly the latter half of this generation came of age during the Great Recession. The economic uncertainties of that time have left an indelible mark.

In fact, the Recession may well have influenced the choice of career path for many new dentists. Dentistry has ranked in the top few professions for a number of years in terms of both income and quality of life.

Generation Y'ers, as a group, are strongly oriented toward financial success and security. They're tech-savvy, unbelievably connected electronically, and ambitious. They're not afraid to innovate in pursuit of their goals.

The internet is constantly changing, and new grads are very comfortable with staying abreast of those changes. But that's just one way they differ from established dentists.

Charting Their Own Paths

For many new Generation Y dentists, a "nontraditional" path to owning their own practices is just fine. They see nothing wrong with working for someone else while they establish themselves in a position of strength before pursuing entrepreneurship.

The enormous dental school debt load I mentioned in the previous chapter just adds to new dentists' drive to succeed. But they're determined to succeed on their own terms, which are very much unlike those of most baby boomers.

It's neither fair nor accurate to attribute exactly the same characteristics to every member of a generation, but we're not interested in every millennial. We're interested in dentists, and for that group, some interesting data are available.

The corporate ladder isn't something most recent graduates are interested in climbing. In fact, a 2014 survey showed that a paltry 13 percent of millennials overall were interested in a traditional corporate career path. Sixty-seven percent were interested in becoming entrepreneurs.

As of a few years ago, entrepreneurial drive to be one's own boss was reported as being higher among male dental school graduates (92 percent) than females (77 percent).

But today women make up nearly half of dental school classes. Guess where most of those women doctors are going to work? You got it: large group practices and corporate dentistry offices.

The 92 percent of male graduates and 77 percent of female graduates who don't particularly feel like working for someone else are paying down their debt with an eye toward opening their own practices. And corporate dentistry is making it easy for new graduates to choose them.

Some dental chains are offering to pay down or even pay off dental school debt – at the time of this writing, Aspen Dental is offering **up to $200,000 in debt payment** for new hires. Midwest Dental is offering **a $30,000 sign-on bonus, relocation, and profit-sharing!**

With those kinds of incentives, even the most entrepreneurial graduates will be hard-pressed to say no to corporate dentistry. You can expect that quite a few will join the corporate ranks ... at least for a while.

Other dental chains are actually funding new dentists who agree to become part of their network. Typically, the dentist will be required to put up around 25 percent of the startup costs, including initial operating capital, and the chain will carry the note once financing is approved.

Don't think this is happening? An article published in May 2016 described the growing impact of corporate dentistry in Texas. The article stated in addition to having a "major" presence at the state dental association annual meeting, well-known chains such as Heartland Dental are **affecting the career paths of newly graduated dentists.** And corporate dentistry will be the winner of this "new" career arc.

The Money Returns

Once those graduates have paid down or paid off their school debt, then what? Those unwilling to have any further association with corporate dentistry have options.

The economy has improved enough since the 2009 crash that private equity groups and venture capitalists are making funds available for these new dentists. For that matter, banks are once again interested in funding new dentists thanks to dentistry's historically low failure rate. As just one example, Bank of America has even put out a financial tip sheet for dental practice startups.

The young, ambitious new dentists are there. The means are there for them to pay off school debt quickly. The money to finance their own practices is there. And those dentists who deferred retirement due to the Great Recession of 2007-2009 are now looking to sell their practices.

According to the ADA Health Policy Institute, the supply of dentists is expected to increase through 2033. And if that's not enough, the growth in practicing dentists will exceed the growth in the U.S. population. That means *fewer* dental patients per practice.

You're looking at more new competition, and those competitors won't be operating on a shoestring budget. You're also looking at a generation that, by all reports, is interested in quick success. That will likely translate into an aggressive marketing approach to attract new patients. Remember, this generation is tech-savvy and probably far more comfortable with online marketing than you are. They essentially grew up in a connected world, and they continue to live there.

New dental schools churning out hungry new dental graduates mean just one thing – war between their practices and yours.

This is not good news for the average independent dental practice. Most practices already have spare capacity, so the presence of one or more new dentists in your market, siphoning away more of your prospects, is likely to hit hard. Hard on you, and hard on your staff. Empty chairs are the bane of every dental practice.

The Second Horseman of War – new dental graduates – is gaining strength. Together with the Conquest-oriented goals of corporate dentistry, you're facing a formidable challenge.

Fighting Back

By way of comfort, let's turn to Sun Tzu again.

Confront them with annihilation, and they will then survive; plunge them into a deadly situation, and they will then live. When people fall into danger, they are then able to strive for victory.

The future of your dental practice is in danger; you are now able to strive for victory. You can strive using the same marketing approach as all the other dentists in your market. Ultimately, though, you'll be defeated no matter how valiant a battle you wage.

Or, y**ou can change the way you wage war** against the practices that would steal your new dental patients.

Do you have the will and the determination to do **whatever it takes** – ethically – to ensure your practice survives?

That different way is the secret weapon I mentioned at the close of the last chapter. It's not for everyone; it requires a special kind of dentist to wield it. If you have the **courage** and the **resolve** to take a different approach than you're used to, you can thrive in spite of the forces against you.

You might be wondering how that could be true. The following excerpted SmartBox blog post from October 2016 will explain.

Your One Advantage over New Dental School Grads

An article in the ADA News touted the expansion of a program designed to prepare those hungry and debt-ridden dental school graduates for the real world.

ADA Success covers such areas as practice management, money management, employment agreements, and finding a job, among others.

One thing that the program doesn't explicitly cover is dental practice marketing. If those new graduates open their own practices, they're going to have learn marketing as they go along. Just like you did, probably.

Think back to when you first hung out your shingle. What was your marketing approach way back then? How did you decide on it?

The odds are that you took a look at what your competitors were doing and did the same. Or, if you were lucky, you had a mentor you could consult for tips and ideas. If you were extraordinarily fortunate, you had the funds to hire a dental marketing firm.

And as one month turned into two, and then into six, you probably found yourself trying to juggle your marketing to produce better results. It's likely that you didn't truly know what parts of your marketing were producing and which weren't.

That leads to the one advantage you enjoy over those new dental school grads. You might think it's that you're established, or that you already have a patient base, or that you have a great location.

No, your one advantage is this: **You already know that your current marketing doesn't work as well as you'd like it to.**

You're reading a blog about dental marketing. If your current program consistently produced all the quality new patients you could handle, you wouldn't need or want to shake things up. You'd be too busy making money.

Instead, you're likely getting a lot of price shoppers and one-and-dones. You may be spending your days on an unending string of drill-and-fills. And you're probably being squeezed by declining insurance reimbursements.

If corporate dentistry is in your area, it's sucking away new patients that you might otherwise have gotten. If it hasn't reached you yet, it will.

Some of those new grads might be moving to your market. That means even more competition for the same pool of dental prospects.

You Have One Advantage. Use It.

If you've been following SmartBox's marketing, you know that we offer a **proven, industry-leading Patient Attraction System™**.

You've probably read or watched testimonials from our dentists who have used our system to attract **more and better patients** and to **get more profits and more freedom** to pursue the cases they love to handle.

Maybe you read where our Elite-level dentists averaged 110 new patient calls a month during the first quarter of this year.

Or you've read about Dr. Raleigh Pioch, who grew his dental practice from $800,000 to **$3.2 million** a year in just six years.

You know three things:

1. Your current marketing doesn't work as well as you'd like.
2. There's a proven **Patient Attraction System™** that is helping dentists on three continents achieve "double-their-practice-or-better" growth.
3. That system is backed by the **SmartBox $10,000 Guarantee™**.

The new graduates and corporate dentistry are **coming for your patients.**

What will you do?

Seize the Power

We still have two more Horsemen to get to know – Famine and Pestilence. Remember – knowledge is power, and with the enormous forces you're facing, you need all the power you can get.

Not-So-Fun Fact:

As of 2015, there were 195,722 dentists working in dentistry in some capacity, according to the ADA Health Policy Institute.

That number is increasing.

3
THE SQUEEZE IS ON

In February 2017, Delta Dental stuck it to dentists in Massachusetts.

Delta's plan to sell lower-cost PPO dental insurance policies, phasing out its Premium policies, is bad news for dentists' incomes. Under its PPO model, dentists will experience a reduction in reimbursement rates **between 20 and 30 percent**.

Delta didn't make the change because it wasn't making money. Instead, Delta wanted to address a "slowdown" in its growth by appealing to cost-conscious consumers and businesses. Or to put it another way, the insurance company is determined to grow at dentists' expense.

This change to reimbursement rates was announced for Massachusetts only, but it's by no means the only time Delta has cut dentists' payments:

- **2011:** Washington dentists experienced a 15 percent reduction.
- **2011:** Idaho was hit with rate reductions up to 13 percent.
- **2012:** New Jersey got off fairly lightly with up to a 5 percent reduction.
- **2012:** Connecticut dentists dodged most of a bullet with a similar 5 percent reduction.
- **2013:** Missouri experienced a 7 percent rate reduction.
- **2017:** After a protracted 3.5-year legal battle, the California Dental Association reached a settlement agreement with Delta over its plans to cut reimbursement rates in that state by 8-12 percent.

I think you're sensing a pattern here, yes?

Delta expects that the existing Premium networks will empty as employers switch to cost-saving policies. Not only will Delta pay less for its PPO policyholders, but dentists will have fewer and fewer Premium patients. That's the Catch-22 for Massachusetts dentists. Those who refuse to agree to Delta's changes will lose patients. Those who do agree will lose money.

Will other dental insurance providers follow Delta's lead? While there's no way to be certain, it seems very likely. According to the ADA, PPO dental networks accounted for nearly **80 percent** of the market as of 2016. That's a powerful incentive for Delta and other insurance companies to continue to squeeze dentists on reimbursements.

The writing is definitely on the wall: your reimbursement for in-network patients, already low, is poised to head **lower**.

According to the ADA's Health Policy Institute, the cost of providing dental care has increased from 2005 to 2014. Dental insurance reimbursements haven't kept pace with that growth. In some cases – perhaps many cases – reimbursements have declined.

And as you've seen, some insurance reimbursements have been **axed**.

As a small business owner, you don't have the leverage to negotiate reimbursement rates unless you're in a strongly underserved market. And maybe not even then. Guess who does have the economic strength to negotiate a better deal from Delta?

But that's not the only challenge you're facing from the Third Horseman.

Passing the Bucks

A lot of online commentary suggests Delta is determined to grow at the expense of dental patients as well as dentists. There are two prongs to this argument.

The first objection is that dentists who agree to the PPO plans are restricted to referring patients to in-network specialists. While those specialists may be competent, the restrictions substitute policy for clinical expertise and judgment about what's best for the patient.

The second objection is a potential downturn in the quality of care. Lower reimbursement rates mean that patients are responsible for a greater portion of the cost of dental work. Dentists may not be able to use the optimal materials for restorations. Cash-strapped patients who would otherwise have work done will defer treatment.

Delta's move encourages price shopping among dental prospects and is likely to result in new patients consulting corporate dental offices.

Cost-conscious dental consumers are looking for "good enough" dental care at the lowest possible price. These patients are **exactly** corporate dentistry's target demographic. Regrettably, many of those corporate practices aren't known for providing quality, appropriate work.

You Can't Sink Fast Enough to Win

As insurance reimbursements drop, many dentists will be tempted to lower their prices – shaving their margins to at least keep the money coming in. But as you've seen, the only winner of a race to the bottom on price is corporate dentistry.

If you're not already seeing dental prospects who want to negotiate the cost of services, you will. And the only way to keep those "hard-core" price shoppers is to agree to perform the services for less.

With lower insurance reimbursements and discounted procedure prices, you'll get less "nourishment" from each "meal." And if you don't get enough nourishment, your practice will starve. That's why decreased insurance reimbursements are **the Third Horseman – Famine.**

There's an old saying: "An army travels on its stomach." If you can't eat, you can't fight, and Conquest and War will triumph.

Unless ...

Fight the Enemy Where They Aren't

Okay, there's actually no such quote in *The Art of War*, so you can relax. But maybe there should be.

Corporate dentistry has staked out the price-conscious, "good-enough" dental consumers. That's about 80 percent of the market. As you've seen, you can't compete for that segment for any length of time and hope to prosper.

What do you think would happen if you fought corporate dentistry where it's *not*?

As we look in depth at the Fourth Horseman, the Death of economic uncertainty, that idea – that *strategy* – will become even more important.

Not-So-Fun Fact:

Delta Dental covers some 74 million people in the U.S.

4
When Things Go Smash ... Again

The stock market is not the economy, but it was hard to believe that in 2008.

The first signs of the Great Recession, as it's come to be called, showed up in 2007, but it wasn't until 2008 that economists realized what was going on.

When the subprime mortgage market collapsed, it took the rest of the economy with it. Unemployment rose to more than 10 percent as some 8 million jobs were lost. Home values crashed 28 percent, and an estimated $16 trillion were erased from household and non-profit assets. According to the Bureau of Labor Statistics, the decline in consumer spending was **the greatest since World War II**.

And dentists felt the pain. Dental incomes had been falling since 2000, and the effects of the Great Recession made the situation far more difficult. Visits, production, and collections declined sharply from 2008 to 2010. Numerous dentists who had planned to retire found their retirement incomes threatened and no ready buyers for their practices, leading many of them to remain in practice to recoup their losses.

Since 2010, dental practice incomes have slowly recovered. But if you think that the financial measures put in place after the Great Recession will prevent another one, you haven't been paying attention.

Loopholes on Loopholes

The Dodd-Frank Wall Street Reform and Consumer Protection Act (Dodd-Frank) of 2010 has never been fully implemented. Some of the regulators who were tasked with writing rules had, or have, considerable bias toward banks. Unrelenting pressure from banking industry lobbyists has watered down some proposed rules and scuttled others.

Numerous derivatives have escaped regulation entirely. And there's considerable sentiment with the current Congress and Administration for repealing Dodd-Frank. That work has already begun as of this writing.

Arguably, the United States remains highly vulnerable to another Great Recession.

There are considerable rumblings among analysts that stocks are overvalued to a greater degree than was true in 2002 and 2008. Taking just one index, the Dow Industrials experienced a classic "double-dip head-and-shoulders" pattern from August 2015 to February 2016. After that telling correction – this is a very well known and used market signal – it continued to march upward. The fundamentals don't look to be in place to support much additional growth, which would lead at the very least to a strong market correction. At worst, things will go smash again.

A Lone Voice

I didn't arrive at this scenario out of thin air. As far back as two years ago, I saw signs of trouble. I shared that information in Patient Attraction Podcast™ 274.

If dental practices are any indication, the U.S. economy is headed for a downturn.

A recent *Bloomberg Businessweek* article caught my attention. The article used four dental indicators to surmise that the American economy may not be headed in the right direction.

First, the fundamentals:

The premise of the article is that when people are uncertain about their economic future, they cut back on dentistry. To measure whether people are cutting back on dentistry, the article's author used data compiled by Sikka Software, which provides business health care applications to small and mid-sized practices, including dentists. The data includes 12,200 American dental practices going back to 2007.

Now for the results.

There are four numbers the article's author uses to show people are cutting back on dentistry.

First, data shows that patients are increasing canceling follow-up appointments. What's more, there has been a precipitous drop over the course of this year.

Second, production during regular hygiene appointments has been volatile this year. So dentists are not consistently doing the cleanings, X-rays, and maintenance they planned during these appointments. That is atypical for economic recovery years, according to the article.

Third, dental practices are planning more treatments than patients are accepting. As dental practices chase higher revenues, they are aggressively scheduling procedures that patients ultimately don't accept.

Finally, patients aren't paying. According to the article, accounts receivable are up 22 percent over the previous year.

Do these four trends represent what you are seeing in your practice? Are you prepared for another economic downturn? What are you doing to make sure you could weather such a storm?

If you're ready to stop leaving your livelihood to chance and to see what a predictable patient attraction system looks like, you should schedule a Patient Attraction System Blueprint™ Session. They are reserved for serious dentists who want to see a patient attraction system that can double their practice.

Better, But Not Good

Since that 2014 podcast, the economic indicators for dentistry have improved slightly, but not evenly. For instance, the ADA Health Policy Institute announced in February 2017 that dental specialists' incomes were stagnant.

But remember that the data referenced in the podcast was collected **five years** after the onset of the Great Recession.

Dentistry is not an industry that rebounds quickly. There **will** be another economic downturn, perhaps sooner than you might think.

In October 2016, the *Wall Street Journal* stated that economists think another recession is likely within <u>the next four years!</u>

Recovery for dental practices will be a long time coming. In fact, there are reasons to think that the next time things go smash, it'll be **worse** than the Great Recession.

We've Probably Quit Bailing

If history has shown anything, it's that unregulated markets tend to excess. The unwinding of financial controls will turn loose the "get-everything-you-can-as-fast-as-you-can" financial players. It's only a matter of time before things go smash – again – and the U.S. economy contracts – again. There's no way to be certain that another recession would be fundamentally deeper than the last one. Regardless, it won't be pretty with the forces currently in play.

It's doubtful that the current Administration will have the desire or the will to bail out the big banks if they fail again. Should the major banks be allowed to go under, the country will be a very long time digging out of its new financial hole. Could you continue to operate your practice if your receipts fell by **20 to 30 percent, or even more, and stayed there?**

If your eyes have begun to glaze over from all this financial talk, relax – it's done. What's not over is that dentists have **a really large axe** hanging over their heads – the threat of another recession that may last for a very long time.

And that recession will take place in a perfect storm of adverse conditions – corporate dentistry, new dental graduates, and declining reimbursements.

The effects on dentists of even a relatively mild recession will be amplified by Conquest, War, and Famine. People haven't forgotten the Great Recession, and they'll be watching. Even rumors of another recession could have a negative impact on your visits, production, and collections. Patients who might have planned on having work done may decide to defer treatment to hoard money against potential job loss.

And this could go on for five years, or even 10.

That's why economic uncertainty is **the Fourth Horseman – Death.**

By this time, you probably think that I'm beating a dead horse, as the saying goes. These horses, and their riders, are anything **but** dead. They're alive, they're in motion, and they're coming for **your** livelihood.

Any one of the Four Horsemen of Dentistry could severely damage your practice and your financial future. To preserve your livelihood in the face of threats from all sides, you'll have to do something different from what you've been doing.

Are You Confident Enough?

I know that suggesting you abandon the marketing approach that got you here is a big ask. I know that not every dentist will have the confidence to take that scary step into the unknown.

There's an old story about a guy who fell off a cliff but managed to grab a tree growing out of sheer rock. His grip began to weaken, and he cried out, "Oh, God, save me!"

A booming voice answered, "Let go of the branch, my son!"

The guy looked down – several thousand feet – then looked up and asked, "Anybody else up there?"

That joke's so old it has whiskers, but it makes a couple of points. First, I'm not the head honcho – I'm just a guy with a **proven** system for getting more and better patients.

Second, if you're in what looks like a no-win situation, **you've got to change how you respond to and approach that situation**. Just like gravity, the forces in play are too big to ignore and far too powerful to change.

If you're not feeling confident, let me share some advice from our Patient Attraction Podcast™ series. This is episode 188 (we're well over a thousand, right now!), and it speaks to what being a confident dentist actually means.

9 Traits of Confident Dentists

Since I started SmartBox, I've talked with untold numbers of dentists. I've talked with millionaires with multiple locations, and I've met guys so far in debt they thought they would never get out. I've seen successful dentists and I've seen dentists who ultimately failed. I've seen plenty of guys in between.

One thing that stands out to me is that confidence breeds success.

So here is a list of my own observations and those of experts in the shared traits of confident dentists:

1. **Confident dentists are more worried about doing what is right than being right.**
   This means a confident dentist can give an initial diagnosis or propose a solution and then change his or her mind or go a different direction. Confidence isn't defending your decisions to the end; confidence is being secure enough to do the right thing even if it wasn't your original plan.

2. **Confident dentists listen more than they speak.**
   A confident dentist doesn't have to impress you with what he knows. He wants to know what his patient wants or what his advisor can tell him that he may not know. Confidence is knowing that you know but not having to show it off.

3. **Confident dentists don't have to be the center of attention.**
   A confident dentist is happy when others get credit. That may mean a staff member or a patient. A confident dentist doesn't care who gets the credit as long as there is a reason for credit to be given.

4. **Confident dentists don't have to know everything.**
   Asking for help or information isn't a sign of weakness. It actually shows that the dentist has enough confidence is his knowledge or her knowledge that they can acknowledge what they don't know. This can be shown in practicing dentistry and relying on a colleague or mentor for expertise in a procedure. It also can go in his business practice in asking someone like me to help build his practice.

5. **Confident dentists strive to grow their practice.**
   A confident dentist doesn't restrict how big his practice can get. This means there are no limits to how much success the confident dentist sees for himself.

6. **Confident dentists don't have to put others down to lift themselves up.**
   This, like many others on the list, extends beyond dentists. Tearing down other people, whether that is competitors,

acquaintances, or whomever, doesn't build anyone up. Confident dentists don't need to do that.

7. **Confident dentists aren't afraid to be themselves.**
I see this in video especially. We want dentists to be themselves on camera so that patients can get to know them and get to like them. But some dentists want to put on a persona to be more professional or serious. Confident dentists are comfortable being who they are. Being yourself is a great way to attract patients that you will mesh with.

8. **Confident dentists own their mistakes.**
A confident dentist knows that we are not defined by our mistakes. Being wrong about a treatment option or a business decision does not cost a dentist self-esteem. Acting like he wasn't wrong costs a dentist esteem. A confident dentist know that he gains self-esteem by acknowledging he was wrong and making it right.

9. **Finally, confident dentists see challenges as opportunities.**
A confident dentist knows he has the talent to be a good dentist. He just needs to get the right combination of ingredients to make his practice thrive. This confidence comes from his willingness to change and adapt his practice to better attract patients.

You need confidence in what you do and how you do it. You also need confidence in how you're going about attracting new patients.

Confidence Breeds Success

You're an accomplished professional, but you're **not** a professional marketer. You didn't go to school for that, and it wasn't in your dental school curriculum. You've maybe made some mistakes along the way, either by doing your own marketing or trusting that a traditional marketing company would get you the new patients you needed. If so, those mistakes don't define you. Let it go.

Yes, the prospect of taking a step into the unknown – letting go of the branch – can be unnerving. What's required is confidence, and that confidence will come from learning exactly how you can prepare your practice for the dental apocalypse and thrive in spite of it.

I'm confident that once you've finished this book, **you'll** have the confidence "to change and adapt your practice to better attract patients."

One last nod to Sun Tzu:

> **In the midst of chaos, there is also opportunity.**

FUN FACT!!

If you know what you're doing, the corporate dentistry marketing machine has an enormous weakness it can never overcome.

– Dr. Michael Abernathy
FOUNDER, SUMMIT PRACTICE SOLUTIONS

5
The Patient Attraction System™

Back in "the day," the only forms of electronic marketing were radio and television. Telemarketing hadn't been invented, and the internet hadn't been conceived of.

Generally, state regulatory boards didn't allow dentists to advertise. Dentists used the tools that were available to them and slugged it out for new patients through Yellow Pages ads. Personal word-of-mouth recommendations were crucial for practices to get new patients.

As the state regulations on advertising gradually loosened, dentists added newspaper ads, direct mail postcards, billboards, and all the other familiar "traditional" forms of advertising. Some dentists, perhaps out of desperation, may have resorted to using sidewalk "sandwich boards."

Those advertisements gradually evolved to focus primarily on price. In other words, dentists began chasing patients through their advertising.

One tongue-in-cheek definition of tradition is, "If enough people do a stupid thing, and enough time passes between that thing and its original stupidity, then that is tradition."

It's tongue in cheek because there are *always* reasons for traditions to form. What renders traditions irrelevant is the simple passage of time and the changes that time brings.

That Was The Day That Was

A lot of time has passed since "the day." Marketing has been transformed in ways that dentists back then couldn't have imagined. And yet, most dentists' marketing today is still based on the idea of "chasing" patients by advertising discounts and specials. It doesn't matter whether the advertising is print or electronic – the bait on the hook is low price.

That, sir or madam, is stupidity. It makes no sense to compete against all the other dental practices in your market by doing exactly what they do. It makes less than no sense to continue doing that when you know you'll get *less and less* in return for your hard work and dedication to your patients.

I remember the brainwashing I received.

It started the day I tried to hand out my business card and got a lecture from the "old guard" about why those activities were "beneath us" in the dental profession.

Glad I never listened!

– Dr. Darold Opp
ABERDEEN, SOUTH DAKOTA

We're Going Nowhere, but We're Getting There Fast

Advertising requires fairly frequent variation to prevent your "customers" from becoming numb to your offers. That makes a traditional dental advertising approach much like a treadmill – you have to keep going and going over exactly the same ground to make it work.

If you stop to think about it, you're not really "going" anywhere. Treadmills are great for some things, but attracting new dental patients isn't one of them.

The monthly advertising treadmill also can be a source of stress for busy dentists. It's time-consuming to try to figure out this month's offer and to design your ad. After all, there are only so many services you can discount. You also have to keep track of what you've used recently, assess how well each ad worked, and try to do better than last month. Not to mention paying for your advertising.

And all the time you know that with decreasing reimbursements, marketing on price is a race to the bottom. Even then, you may not get the new patients you need, but you can work yourself half to death trying.

With the Horsemen coming to town, expect that stress factor to jump through the roof.

Fortunately, you can get off the advertising treadmill and leave the stupidity to others.

Some of the advertising I've done in the past was more offer-driven, free exam, X-ray kind of thing.

When you bring patients in that way, you're chasing them for the next offer or they're chasing you for the next offer, all the way down the line.

– Dr. James Kiehl
NEW HAMPSHIRE

It's a Brave New (Wired) World

The increasing dominance of the internet in everyday life has changed how dentists should market to patients.

Most people these days – at a bare minimum, 80 percent – begin their search for a dentist online. Only the few, the proud, or perhaps the old even have a phone book with Yellow Pages.

The beauty of using the internet to market your practice is that it can convey so much more useful information than even an entire ad campaign. Most dentists, though, still focus on specials, discounts, and coupons in their online advertising. They're doing the **same old thing** with a much more powerful and flexible medium.

Does that make any sense to you?

Dentists who want to attract new patients through online marketing have to take into account that today's dental prospects are different. People born after 1980 or so have grown up in an atmosphere of high electronic stimulation – multiple radio channels, cable TV, chat boards, social media, and so on. Those high stimulation levels and easy access to information have changed the way people respond to marketing.

Studies show that younger people would rather watch short videos than read short articles. That doesn't mean online articles, blog posts, and social media entries aren't important. It means that today's online marketing demands a coordinated, broad-based approach that presents useful information to prospects in the ways they'll respond to best. A simple price-based advertising approach just isn't going to cut it.

All Clicks Are Not Created Equal

The fact that advertising based on price is a downward spiral doesn't stop a lot of dentists from trying, though. Some of them are taking a stab at internet marketing by spending a bundle on pay-per-click (PPC) price-based advertising.

It sounds so good, doesn't it? Put your ad up online and pay nothing unless someone clicks on it. As with everything else related to marketing in the connected age, PPC is a lot more complex than it sounds. Before you take a dive into that pool, you'd do well to check out what it takes to stay afloat.

Let's Hear from an Expert

Sam Smock, SmartBox's Digital Marketing Director, joined me for the October 2016 episode of our Inside Patient Attraction™ webinars. Sam's a big proponent of PPC advertising but cautions that there are a lot of considerations to take into account if pay-per-click is going to pay off for dentists. What follows is a lightly edited transcript of that episode.

Inside Patient Attraction™ October 2016

Colin: Welcome to Inside Patient Attraction. Today we're going to cover a very controversial topic talking about pay-per-click and if it works or doesn't work for dentists to attract new patients into their practices. A lot of dentists are doing it, a lot of dentists aren't. We're going to hit all the high points today. Also, I want to talk about something not known: how pay-per-click can actually help your organic SEO rankings improve.

I'm Colin Receveur here with Sam, our Digital Marketing Manager. Welcome on board for this edition of Inside Patient Attraction.

Sam: Hi, Colin. Thanks for having me.

Colin: Glad to have you here. We're going to talk today about pay-per-click, everything that you need to know about how to attract new patients into your practice with pay-per-click, what it can do for you, what it can't do, how it affects other areas of your marketing, and how you can leverage the data that you get from pay-per-click in other areas. Tell us high-level what are you doing with pay-per-click with dentists right now.

Sam: We're using pay-per-click to really grow that lead pipeline. It's a great way to immediately attract leads for people searching for relevant information that they can find on your website.

Colin: New patients?

Sam: Absolutely.

Colin: Why do new patients want to click on the paid ads?

Sam: Plenty of reasons. There's a lot of merit to being right at the very top of that search results page, and that's a big part of our pay-per-click strategy.

Colin: If you're not first, you're last.

Sam: It's how the wisdom goes.

Colin: When you're looking at how you get to be first in pay-per-click, tell me a little bit about how that formula – a lot of people think it's an auction, it's a bidding process – how does that work to get up to the top?

Sam: Just like any auction, what it is, is the advertiser who's willing to pay the highest price for the click will win that click. It also goes into other things like your quality score, the relevance of your website – there's tons of factors that are involved, and that's what we do here at SmartBox to make sure we're the most effective with our pay-per-click.

Colin: What I found is that a lot of dentists don't know about pay-per-click, and something I want to talk about today is quality score, because that's kind of a big unknown for dentists. If a dentist asks you, "How do you define quality score?" what would you tell them that is?

Sam: One word, Colin: relevance.

Colin: Relevance is king, as Gary Vaynerchuk says.

Sam: Absolutely.

Colin: Relevance – tell me, how does quality score get figured into the pay-per-click process? Tell me a little bit about that formula.

Sam: Google, they want to send search traffic to the best possible place so they are totally focused on that user experience. If they see that your website has the most relevant content to what that user is searching, you're going to get a better quality score, and that can help you in tons of ways with your overall pay-per-click strategy.

Colin: Tons of ways being lower click prices and higher ranking?

Sam: Absolutely.

Colin: I've got a great infographic that I've used that shows the formula back and forth, and it's pretty simple: bid price times quality score equals your ranking plus how much you pay. A lot of dentists don't realize that you have to optimize for SEO and you have to optimize for pay-per-click. A lot of guys just do pay-per-click and they don't realize there's an optimization component behind it.

Sam: Right.

Colin: I know the rule of thumb. I've always told our docs that if your pay-per-click people don't have access to your website or they are not optimizing your website, you're probably paying out the wazoo.

Sam: Most likely.

Colin: What else? What are you finding is best practices in pay-per-click right now? What are you finding is effective for getting new patients?

Sam: Showing these people the benefits of what you offer. You have a very small space to convince them why they should click on your ad, and I think you need to lead with the most important things that you think would attract those new patients.

Colin: Once they click on the ad, tell me about the process that you're walking these patients through.

Sam: This goes back to the relevance. They enter in a search, and the ad displays and it should be relevant to what they are looking for. Then what happens, once they get that click, they go to your website. Now, if you've done your homework, they are going to a page that is completely relevant to what they are searching for. Again, it's that user experience that Google is very, very interested in. In fact, that's mostly what they focus on these days.

Colin: You're just not putting an ad out and dropping them onto the home page of their website when they click on that pay-per-click ad?

Sam: Right.

Colin: That would be completely irrelevant. They are clicking on a specific ad and then you're dumping them onto a generic – the home page of your website or some generic page.

Sam: Right, these users are wanting to find exactly what they are looking for right when they are looking. They don't want to navigate, they don't want to look too hard for what they are finding. They want to see it right when they get to your website.

Colin: Is there any difference in market areas that you see for some dentists that are doing pay-per-click effectively, or better than other market areas?

Sam: Sure, that comes down to competition. Larger markets are always going to have much, much higher competition, so what does that do? That drives your cost per click up. It's just a hard fact, and what we do is through our optimization, we really find ways to be efficient with those budgets especially in those tougher markets.

Colin: How do you do that?

Sam: Keywords – we look at the keywords most likely to convert. We look at things like quality score that try to help us lower that cost per click, and then we also really try to make sure we provide that great user experience because if we do have a limited budget, we want all of those users who click on our ads to actually be more likely to convert.

Colin: By conversion, what do you mean?

Sam: New patients, either phone call, web inquiry, coming right in to visit your office.

Colin: Something that's putting butts in the chair.

Sam: That's right. That's the whole goal.

Colin: That's the dentist's goal, too. A lot of questions that I see from dentists, they are talking about using SEO versus pay-per-click. How would you weigh those? If you can briefly tell me, what do you see is the primary differences or the strengths maybe, or weaknesses of both?

Sam: Sure. The old wisdom goes that SEO is the marathon and PPC is the sprint.

Colin: I like that.

Sam: Your entire marketing plan should be basically your SEO strategy, and that's very long term. It takes time, it takes lots of visits, lots of data to aggregate. Pay-per-click is immediate, you get immediate data, you can analyze it, you can see what works, and then you can take that data and leverage it to aid with your SEO strategy.

Colin: When you start and launch a pay-per-click campaign for a dentist, how long until that dentist actually starts getting phone calls and seeing results?

Sam: It could be immediate. The very first day you go live with PPC, you could get a new patient phone call that same day.

Colin: When you're launching these pay-per-click campaigns, how much prep time do you spend going in and looking and building that campaign out?

Sam: It take some time. We like to look at the market, we like to look at what that dentist offers, we like to look at the website, and we just want to make sure we come up with the best strategy to provide that good user experience and make sure we're attracting the right type of traffic that is going to turn into the best leads for that dentist.

Colin: Best kind of patients.

Sam: Best kind of patients.

Colin: Now, I've heard you mention several times the best user experience. How would you describe that? When you use that phrase, tell me what you envision with best user experience, because that seems to be a really important staple of what you're talking about here and what you're building.

Sam: Sure. User experience – are the users finding what they are looking for, and are they finding it easily, and is your site easy to use? Are you giving them the information they want? You see, Google is basically like your friend who's referring you to a business. They want to give you a good referral, a good reference. They want to send you to the best place because ultimately that helps Google, because Google wants these people to come back to Google.

Colin: So they can make more ad revenue.

Sam: Exactly.

Colin: Sure.

Sam: Google has a very, very vested interest in making sure the places they send traffic is going to provide that best user experience.

Colin: How does Google measure that?

Sam: They have algorithms that we can't even fathom.

Colin: They are looking at things like time on site, bounce rate – the same statistics that we're gathering from our analytics Google is looking at as well to measure the user experience, to measure quality score.

Sam: Exactly. Google is taking a look at the same data we're looking at with what users do when they come to the site, how easily they are finding the information, and where they go on the site to determine whether that site has that good user experience that we're looking for.

Colin: When Google is determining what the consumer wants, what the new patient wants, is there any specific content that they like to see on websites?

Sam: It really depends on what type of search they are performing. Usually what they are going to be looking for is exactly what that keyword, that search term that they've entered into the search engine is usually going to be the top thing that you're going to want to show them.

Colin: You want to make sure if they are searching for All-on-4® dental implants that you're driving them to a landing page within your website that is about All-on-4 protocols and dental implants specifically with all the information below. You don't want to drop them onto just a generic landing page because then that's irrelevant for that user.

Sam: Precisely, and that is exactly what the search engine wants you to do.

Colin: Google shook up the pay-per-click here recently and changed how the pay-per-click ads are actually displayed on the search engine result pages. Tell me a little bit about what you found and how that affected things.

Sam: Yes, Google made a change recently where they got rid of the right-hand rail ads and they added this fourth ad spot at the top of the search engine results page. The results of this are yet to be determined, but it's one of those things where some people might say they've reduced the amount of ads on the page so they think competition is going to get tougher. Where some people see challenge, other see opportunity. We look at that, as now there's four spots at the top where there used to be three.

Colin: Have you seen any increases or decreases in keyword prices?

Sam: That hasn't really been affected, but what I've noticed is that you are now able to be on the top four results for a much more effective price than you could when there were three spots.

Colin: Because you have four spots, you have an extra spot at the top.

Sam: Yeah.

Colin: What about bidding on long-tail versus short-tail keywords? And talking about – I've heard the "broad versus phrase" match thrown around. Tell me a little bit about how you figure out what keyword you actually want to buy and how that process goes.

Sam: You want to look at the search intent. When people enter these long-tail type of keywords, they are looking for something very specific. If you offer that specific thing they are looking for, you make that part of your strategy. If you are just looking for high volume, say you have a big budget to play with, you're going to just want to do a broad match, you're going to want to go after everything, and that's where optimization comes in to really understand who your customers are, what you're offering, and then tailor the strategy accordingly.

Colin: What about targeting these ads? How specific can you get with local targeting, or geo-fencing as I've heard it called, or using local keywords?

Sam: The old wisdom goes, the best leads are always in your backyard. Google knows this. Localized search is becoming very, very important, especially with the emergence of mobile devices. Lot of marketers are focusing very heavily on what we're calling hyper-local targeting. It's just that old wisdom of going after those leads right in your backyard that are most likely to convert.

Colin: What about for large-case doctors that are looking to branch out of their local market area? How can you target that for, say, my dad, Dr. Receveur – he markets from Indianapolis to Cincinnati, Chicago, all around within 200 miles. How do you handle that with a pay-per-click campaign?

Sam: It just goes back to your strategy. You look at all these geographies you want to target, and you can really get on a micro-level of these geographies. You can basically apply that hyperlocal strategy to a more broad area. You're still getting that hyperlocal data and information and strategy, but you're targeting a wider area casting a wider net for more leads.

Colin: If a dentist, for instance, decides he wants to target some city or a larger area, he simply draws a line around that area and applies the strategy, and you can drop ads all over and saturate that market area online, so to speak.

Sam: You absolutely can do that.

Colin: Awesome. What about ... I mean, Google can't be the only player out there in the game with AdWords with their pay-per-click. What else are you doing that's working in the paid marketing world?

Sam: Sure. Right now, Google is king. It's definitely the most widely used search engine, but there are certainly other players in the game, Yahoo, Bing. Both of those engines do offer paid search ads, and there are very valuable audiences using those engines.

Colin: Any differences in demographics between the different search engines?

Sam: Bing tends to skew maybe a little bit older. Also, they are seeing that younger people are using it more and more, but still Google is the number one player in the game right now.

Colin: Google seems to have the middle of the road whereas Bing has the top and the bottom of the age group when you're looking at the spread.

Sam: That's what we're seeing right now.

Colin: How about times of the day? I mean, if you can be so specific with who you're showing and where you're showing and getting these results so quickly, what about showing ads at certain times of the day?

Sam: Sure. In the marketing world, that's what we would call day parting. What we do with our strategies, we look at the times of day where the most searches happen. Also the times of day more likely generate those new phone calls, those new patient phone calls. We like to tailor our strategy to where we're serving our paid search ads in those most relevant times of the day. You can target that to the hour of the day. It's very specific.

Colin: If you had a dentist that, say, didn't want to get emergency patients on Saturday night and midnight on Wednesday, you could literally just turn off all the advertisements except during the hours that the dentist wanted to be seen?

Sam: That's right.

Colin: If he's, say, an implant dentist that we see a lot of implant leads come in late at night for information and educational-based material that leads to our patient interaction system that nurture marketing within Infusionsoft® and else, you could leave those ads on for that implant dentist because that's a very lucrative time for him to be capturing those leads.

Sam: That's right, Colin. You bring up a very good point when we talk about search intent. We definitely use time of day to really factor into our strategy around what these people are searching for and when they might be performing that search, all with the idea of the conversion. That phone call, that action that they are going to take, that's going to lead to them becoming a new patient.

Colin: Talking about these top four positions, I assume if you're in the bottom paid ads for Google you're probably not getting found a lot, nobody looks at the bottom of the page, right?

Sam: Right.

Colin: If you're in the top four, any data that you've seen that shows if one through four, I mean, I know the common logic is number one is always best, but what are you seeing in the data, what are you looking for?

Sam: Sure, everyone wants to be in that number one spot. I haven't met a dentist yet who has turned away a patient because they clicked on a third-place ad, but seriously, obviously you need to be in the top four to play. There are other enhancements you can do to your ad to really help you win that click. While first-place ranking is always great, it may not be the number one deciding factor of who actually wins that click. We like to be in the top four no matter what.

Colin: What are the enhancements you just mentioned?

Sam: Google has rolled out all types of enhancements that you can make to ads so you can give users the option of clicking on certain pages of your website, your About Us, your Contact Us, you can display your phone number, your address, and that really helps with that local search and really was helping that person make that quick decision to click on your ad versus the competition's ad.

Colin: To put it in Yellow Pages terms, it's the bold, the color, the bigger ad that you can show to give you preferential visibility versus everybody else that may just have a plain listing.

Sam: You're right. All these theories really tie back to just basic traditional marketing. It's just that it now is on this new technology.

Colin: You got to get the eyeballs on you.

Sam: Absolutely.

Colin: When you're looking at, let's say you have a dentist in Chicago. Chicago is a huge city. We have several clients there. When you're looking at Chicago and you're working with a dentist on building out a pay-per-click campaign, let's talk a little bit about market share and how many searches are going on and how do you approach, what is the potential upside for a dentist doing this campaign? How many new patients can they get from doing a campaign?

Sam: Sure. Impression share is a very big component of the strategy we do before we build a campaign. We look at how many searches are going on in the area, how much that traffic typically cost, and we determine about how much market share search share that doctor can expect to gain with their budget. With more search share comes more eyeballs, and that leads to more new patients. That's a big part of our optimization and our strategic process.

Colin: Upfront, you're able to tell a dentist that, hey, if you build this campaign in pay-per-click with Google, you can take 30 or 50 or dominate them with 80 percent of all the available searches that are happening within this radius.

Sam: That's right. What that means is maybe you're not winning that click, but your ad is showing up 20, 30, 80 percent of the time depending on what your search share is. There is incredible value in that.

Colin: That's powerful. I mean, that's showing you what's your potential, how many people. This isn't just the newspaper sending out a 150,000-impression circulation. This is actually how many people are actually searching within a radius for a need that they have in real time, and you're able to say that we can saturate that at 50 percent saturation, 80 percent, a 100 percent saturation. You're delivering your ads in real time to a person in need.

Sam: Certainly. In larger markets, that is much more efficient from a budget perspective than many traditional medias.

Colin: Where you're build on impression share and not actual action that's taken on your ad using pay-per-click, you only pay when you play. You don't pay for impressions. A million people can see your paid ads, but if nobody likes what you're selling or what you're doing, if they don't like what you're about, then they don't click, and you pay nothing.

Sam: Exactly, that is one crucial component of pay-per-click and you just hit on it. You do not pay unless someone clicks on your ad.

Colin: I've heard concerns before about click fraud where maybe the competitor down the road is clicking on your ad a thousand times. How does Google handle that?

Sam: Click fraud is a huge concern and Google is very, very attuned to that because it will affect their revenue stream. They have measures in place to really take a look at what's happening and make sure that this click fraud isn't really affecting your budgets too much.

Colin: Essentially, if I click on the same ad twice in a row, Google's algorithms are going to pick me up and not charge that person who's ad I clicked on that kind of locks them out?

Sam: They are, they are going to know that you have clicked from the same IP address twice so you, maybe someone who doesn't have the right search intent. You may be trying to do something that isn't going to help Google and isn't going to help the advertiser.

Colin: Even if I go home and I have a different IP address, I'm still logged into my Google account when I click on the ad. They still know who you are.

Sam: That's right, they do.

Colin: Big Brother following you around.

Sam: That's right.

Colin: Let's talk about ROI. We've talked about all the mechanics of this pay-per-click. We've talked about how it works and how we do it, how you set it up, and what it does. Let's get down to the meat and potatoes of what it really does for dentists. How do you measure ROI?

Sam: We measure ROI with tracking numbers we put on our landing pages. We listen to every phone call, we see what kind of leads are coming in, and we tie that back to the marketing and the paid search strategy.

Colin: When you're tracking these calls, how does that equate into success for the dentist?

Sam: We are looking at how many new patients are calling. Whether they are scheduling, what they are scheduling for, we get feedback from our doctors to see how these patients are coming in and how they are finding them.

Colin: You've been in digital media for years and years, and you've been on board here for a while, but in your past experience with digital, how do they judge ROI for pay-per-click and how's that different from how we do it here at SmartBox?

Sam: You know, in the past we looked at some high-level metrics, click-through rates, conversions. Here at SmartBox, we're a little bit different. We are listening to all the phone calls, and we're really focused on the dentist's success and what those phone calls mean in terms of new patients for our dentist.

Colin: Pay-per-click is a waste of money if you're not really scheduling new patients from all your marketing. You have to be scheduling new patients from it, and that's what we do with our pay-per-click here. Our analyst team listens to every call.

Sam: They do, and it's very valuable information that we can use for both our dentist and also for our paid search strategies.

Colin: We've got analytics on the back end. We've got all these different data sets that we look at internally. Tell me what you're looking at there.

Sam: We are looking at what these users do once they come to the website, how much time they spend, where they go, and what they are looking at, and it's all very valuable information for us to determine what's working, maybe what's not working, what might need to change. It really helps with our optimization and our strategy.

Colin: How often are you looking at it?

Sam: Daily, weekly, it's really an ongoing process and never really ends.

Colin: What kind of stuff do you do daily for pay-per-click? I mean, don't you just set it and forget it?

Sam: You should never set and forget a paid search.

Colin: That was a joke. I wanted to elicit a good response from you, but tell me about what you're doing daily. Why do you need to look at it daily?

Sam: You need to look at it daily because you need to know what's going on. If you let it go for a week, a month, you could miss huge things with the data that are happening that could be actionable insights for you. Things like your click-through rate, things like your time on site, things like how much your bid price is. If you're not constantly monitoring these things, you're really going to miss out on potential leads.

Colin: Google could change your quality score from nine to four and your bid price goes up by 250 percent, and all of a sudden you go from getting a 100 leads for a thousand bucks to getting 20 leads for a thousand bucks.

Sam: Right – you don't want to be asleep at the wheel when that's going on.

Colin: Completely agree. Completely agree. Pay-per-click in the mobile environment is, I mean mobile is getting huge now, so how does mobile pay-per-click differ from desktop or other devices when you're running your pay-per-click campaigns?

Sam: The emergence of mobile device usage has really provided marketers with a lot more data around intent and these very localized searches. With intent, a search for a chipped tooth on a mobile device is going to have a way different intent than somebody researching TMJ or sleep apnea. It provided marketers with lots of data on how we can optimize our bids, our day parting, all of those things we talked about earlier, to really streamline your strategy to be the most efficient you can be.

Colin: Then you could actually build out specific pay-per-click campaigns that target only mobile or only not mobile, right?

Sam: That's right, you can even do mobile-only, call-only ads where you're literally displaying your phone number very prominently, and that's going to be great for people who are looking for emergency patients or people who have that very immediate need. You put their phone number right in front of them, they are more likely to give you a phone call.

Colin: Now, I've seen in some other industries, and maybe this isn't really mainstream in dentistry yet, but I've seen where you can actually geo fence an area, you draw a line around an area and you can deliver ads to people as they drive by your office or deliver coupons to them. Have you seen that coming out of dentistry yet?

Sam: Not as much yet, but it's definitely something that's on the rise. It's one of those things that the emergence of this mobile device usage has allowed for, and the future is going to be really interesting with those types of things.

Colin: I imagine once the Meyers and the Walmarts develop and master the technology that it will trickle down from there to us lowly small business folks, right?

Sam: I think so. I think so, we'll let them do the experimenting first and then we'll take advantage.

Colin: When you're building out a pay-per-click campaign and you're working with the other marketing departments here, how do you leverage pay-per-click as a piece of the whole campaign? Tell me a little bit about how pay-per-click fits into the big picture for dental practice.

Sam: That's right; it's very important to realize that pay-per-click should never stand on its own as your go-to marketing strategy. It needs to be a part of an overall comprehensive approach, and it really needs to mirror everything else. Your SEO strategy is really going to be very much the same as your paid search strategy, and it should all tie together and it should really all be centered around that user experience.

Colin: If you're marketing everywhere online, you're dominating the market area, you have more places to be seen.

Sam: That's right. That's still very important, especially with the continual crowding of the online space. You really need to find ways to cut through that clutter.

Colin: Dominating your market area – if it's with pay-per-click or comprehensive campaign, we're here to help. We're going to be here when you're ready to attract more and better patients into your practice. If you want to see what SmartBox and our Patient Attraction Systems™ can do for you, give us a call. We'd love to show you.

Thanks again for being on the show, Sam. I appreciate your time coming in here and sharing this experience and advice for how to make pay-per-click successful with our doctors and my podcast followers. I look forward to seeing awesome things coming from you here in the next few years. Keep moving forward.

The return on investment is a no-brainer for me when a lifetime value of a new patient at a dental office is thousands of dollars.

You get a few new patients per month that you were not getting before, then it pays for itself right there. Everything else is gravy.

– Dr. Matthew Burton
CLEARWATER, FLORIDA

Get Integrated

If you take away one thing from this discussion of pay-per-click advertising, it's that there's **no single magic bullet** for your marketing. It's PPC, and search engine optimization, and content, and advertising – among **many** other things.

A strong, **integrated** online presence is absolutely necessary if you're going to succeed. Today, there's more competition for search engine results placement, for the decreasing attention spans of today's searchers, and for new patients. An increased number of dentists in a market means your prospects have **more provider options** than ever before.

With more options available, **why** should dental prospects pick **you** over any one of your competitors? If you keep advertising on price, they don't really have a reason.

The Dentist as a Commodity

Dentists today are assumed to be competent. You're a *doctor* with a *doctorate* degree, for crying out loud! That diploma speaks volumes about your dedication, accomplishment, and competence.

But then again, every other dentist is a doctor with a doctorate. In that respect, it's a level playing field.

Advertising like everyone else gives your prospects no reason to choose you instead of a competitor. You become "just another dentist." Your dental prospects are likely to see you as a "technician" who deals with teeth instead of as a dental expert and trusted advisor.

Irritating, isn't it? You spent four long years of hard study and practice to learn your profession, and now you're "just another dentist," kind of like "just another ASE-certified auto mechanic." Sad, but true.

You Succeed When You "Do" You

You simply **will not succeed** by marketing like every other dentist does. Why? Because there are more and more dentists all the time! Keep doing what you've always done, and you won't get what you've always gotten – you'll get less!

The idea of differentiating yourself from your competition – standing out – is a cornerstone of the Patient Attraction System™.

The following is combined from two most-watched episodes of SmartBox's Patient Attraction Podcast™, which aired in December 2014. The takeaway here is that you have to stand out, or you should prepare to stand down.

Patient Attraction Podcast™ Episodes 269 & 270

9 Tricks Dentists Should Use to Make Their Marketing Stand Out

Since you've been in dentistry a while, you may have forgotten what it's like for the rest of the world. But to most people, one dentist is just the same as another. That's why you MUST market if you want to attract more and better patients.

So the first thing you have to do is BE INDEPENDENT. That means stepping out of the herd and going a different way. If everyone else in your market talks about how gentle they are, are you going to stand out by saying you're gentle too?

No, of course not.

Instead, highlight your no-wait policy, extended hours or advanced technology.

Obviously don't promote claims you can't support. But if you have something that sets you apart, let the public know.

Second, look to SHAKE THINGS UP. This may mean partnering with an orthodontist or endodontist to come into your practice once or twice a week to expand your services. Or you can use CE hours to learn a new skill or technique, offer a new procedure, or learn to use new equipment.

Then tell people about it. Make sure potential patients know that you can do more than they thought.

Third, REINVIGORATE YOUR BRAND. If you've had the same website for five years, it's time to update. If you've used the same logo and signage since you opened your practice, it may be time to look at that too.

Trends change with time. What once was modern and attractive is now old and dated. Stay current and draw more patients.

Fourth, APPEAL TO A BROAD AUDIENCE. Even if you do niche dentistry, appeal to the broadest market possible. Orthodontists, for instance, need to market to parents with teenage children – that is their bread and butter. But they also should market to young professionals who want less-noticeable methods for straightening teeth and have the income to afford it.

If you are a GP, you need to be marketing to families from the youngest child to the great-great-grandmother. If you only want to see professional women ages 30-40, you're going to have to spend an awful lot of money to capture such a narrow market.

Number 5, BUILD TRUST. There are many ways you can do this:

- Address your patients' needs instead of what you offer.
- Provide useful information before they become your patient.
- And the best way is to use video.
    - When a potential patient watches you on video, he or she can see your mannerisms, hear your voice, and get to know you.
    - Video establishes trust as no other medium can.

Next, is LOCATION, LOCATION, LOCATION. I don't mean your physical location, though having a nice building that is easy to reach with plenty of parking is certainly a plus. I mean put your marketing message where people are looking. In the 21st century, that means on the web. In the age of smartphones and 24/7 internet access, when was the last time you looked in a phone book for information?

Research shows that 85 percent of customers are looking for local businesses online. If you want new patients to find you, you have to have a *strong* web presence.

The number 7 way to enhance your marketing is to THINK LONG-TERM. Forget coupons (short-term). Build relationships through email marketing (long-term). Forget gimmicks (short-term). Provide information through content (long-term).

If you use specials and discounts to bring in patients, they'll leave you the next time somebody offers a better special or discount.

Eighth, KNOW YOUR PATIENTS' NEEDS. I touched on this a second ago in building trust. Address what is important to them, not what is important to you. Prospects don't care if you use digital X-rays. They do care that they are exposed to less radiation. So don't market your digital X-ray machine. Market that you can expose them to 90 percent less radiation.

And finally, ACT NOW. Start small, but start. Start slow, but start. Whatever you do, start.

It's Time for a Change

If you're going to stop chasing patients like everyone else, you have to fundamentally change how patients perceive you. With a "systems-based" approach to patient attraction, you can strategically position yourself as not just another dentist but as THE trusted dental expert and advisor in your prospects' minds.

You stop **chasing** patients and start **attracting** them.

This approach produces a number of benefits.

1. Prospective patients perceive you and your practice as *the only logical choice* to provide dental care and to solve their dental problems. That sets you apart from your competition. You're no longer in the commodity category.

2. Patients' resistance to fees is drastically minimized. You can sell your case solutions more easily and minimize patient bargaining.

3. You're in command of your market segment. In any given market, there are some 20 percent of patients who have the discretionary funds to pay more for a dentist they trust and view as an expert. Those people aren't corporate dentistry's demographic – they aren't price- or insurance-driven – but they certainly are your demographic. These patients aren't likely to defer dental care or procedures in an economic downturn.

   That 20 percent market segment is *your* insurance against the Four Horsemen. And you've been trying to chase them on price.

4. Corporate dentistry can't compete with a well-designed and -implemented **Patient Attraction System™ (PAS)**. Corporate dental patients are unlikely to see the same dentist twice, given the high turnover in personnel. And there's anecdotal evidence to suggest that more established corporate dentists, under pressure to produce, pull strings in scheduling to get lower-value cases assigned to newer dentists. Corporate can't compete on trust, because it doesn't engender any.

A **Patient Attraction System™** is an integrated approach to getting increasing numbers of qualified new dental patients over time. Dentists who use a PAS can get off the monthly advertising treadmill, get back to doing what they love, and have more and better patients.

The PAS is composed of The Four Pillars, and we'll look at each of those in the following chapters.

Before we do, here's another thought from Sun Tzu.

Nah, just kidding. We're beyond that now.

Survival Strategies

1. Stop chasing patients by advertising like everybody else.

2. Stand out from your competitors, or prepare to stand down.

3. SEO is crucial, involved, and DIFFICULT. Don't try this at home.

4. If you have the time to try doing SEO yourself, you don't have **nearly** enough patients.

5. Be careful who you choose to handle SEO. Not all SEO is created equal, just like a $500 crown vs. a $1,500 crown.

6. Don't fall for the hype; magic marketing bullets don't exist.

7. Your success – your practice's survival – depends on having an integrated system to attract new dental patients.

> As it turns out, what you don't know about patient attraction CAN hurt you!
>
> – Dr. Woody Oakes
> PRESIDENT, THE PROFITABLE DENTIST & EXCELLENCE IN DENTISTRY

6

THE FIRST PILLAR: ATTRACTION

This was before my time, but one of our SmartBox associates tells me that there used to be commercial fishing lakes. Anyone with a fishing license could toss a line in the water, but the lake owners specified what kind of bait and hooks they could use.

So, some weekends, there'd be a hundred or more people on the banks of a relatively small lake, all plugging away with exactly the same lures, trying to catch the same fish.

I'm willing to bet that some of those fishermen cheated.

Competing for the same limited pool of dental prospects in the same way as everyone else is a losing proposition. When you're facing the Four Horsemen of Dentistry, it's an approach that leads in just one direction: **downward**.

Chasing dental prospects through advertising is a hit-or-miss proposition. Not everyone in your market is in need of a cleaning, cosmetic dentistry, orthodontia, or implants in a given month or even in a single quarter. No matter what specials or discounts you're offering at any one time, you'll only appeal to a subset of your market. That's part of the reason why advertising is a treadmill; you've got to keep going after the patients who didn't relate to the offer in your last ad.

As you've learned, advertising on price pegs you squarely as a commodity "discount" dentist. There's one subset of patients in your market who **doesn't want** and **won't visit** a discount dentist. Those are the patients with the discretionary income to pay **more** for a dental expert they **like, relate to, and trust.**

You can't be the trusted expert and the discount dentist. There's a huge disconnect between the two ideas. The **20 percent** of patients who are willing to pay more for a dentist they like, trust, and relate to simply won't respond to price offers.

That leaves you getting discount patients from your advertising. And working harder and longer.

Enough with the Traditional Approach, Already

A strategic approach to attracting patients offers many benefits compared to chasing prospects through advertising.

A **Patient Attraction System™** works constantly to attract new patients, and **better** patients, over time. Without having to continue running on the advertising treadmill, you'll potentially appeal to all the prospects in your market who are appropriate for the services you offer. What's more, your prospects will be convinced that you are **the** dentist for them. When the time is right – when they've decided to have that elective procedure, or they're experiencing a dental emergency – it's your number they'll call.

The Patient Attraction System™ turns every aspect of your marketing into a cohesive, integrated whole to accomplish just one thing – to put more patient butts in your chairs.

When you're not on the monthly advertising treadmill, you're free to actually make money by treating patients. And isn't that why you went to dental school in the first place – to help people by solving their dental problems and to make money doing it?

There's another benefit to positioning yourself as the only logical choice. Once people view you as the trusted, relatable dental expert, their resistance to the cost of procedures is minimized. You'll sell your case solutions far more easily.

With a Patient Attraction System™, you'll enjoy more patients, more profits, and the freedom to handle more of the cases you love to do.

> It's kind of surprising to me already to see how many people just find you on Google.
>
> It's like, well, if you're not on Google, you're not listed, you're not anywhere.
>
> – Corey Hurcomb
> TULIP TREE DENTAL CARE, SOUTH BEND, INDIANA

Nuts, Bolts, and Linchpins

Your dental website is the linchpin of your Patient Attraction System™. Regardless of how they initially find you, dental prospects will visit your website to seek out specific answers for their needs. Your website contains more information about you, your practice, and the solutions you offer for dental problems than any other part of your marketing. In fact, your website is often the last stop for prospects before they pick up the phone to book an appointment.

What's more, your website is where prospects go to find out what your current patients think about you and your practice.

In the Patient Attraction System™, every aspect of your marketing – social media, blog, videos, and, yes, advertising, works to influence prospects to visit your website. And the system's designed to position you as exactly what your better prospects are looking for – a trusted, relatable dental expert.

Get Found by Your Prospects

It's crucial to your success that your website be highly visible during organic search. All dentistry is local, and Google's search results these days are personalized for the searcher, including geographically where that makes sense.

Google is still the dominant search engine by far, and Google has its own rules as to what kind of content it favors in its search results. Google changed the format of its search results page to feature a few of the most highly ranked pages. The competition for placement on the first page of search results has gotten fierce in the last few years, and there's every sign that the competition is only going to intensify.

You can't afford to let your competitors **claim-jump** your spot on this page.

But to make it to the first page of Google search results, and stay there, your website needs state-of-the-art search engine optimization (SEO) and a whole lot more.

If you have an interest in and aptitude for website search engine optimization, you could handle it yourself. But we're talking hours and hours of staying hunched over a computer – not just once, but on an ongoing basis. There are compelling reasons why that's not the best use of your time.

A lot of patients that were coming in were saying that they found us on the internet.

Or I'll ask. I had somebody the other day, I asked, "How did you find me?" They said, "I Googled the best dentist in Belleville." And I said, "Well, you got to the right place, it worked."

The last six months, six to eight months, have been very exceptional.

– Dr. Thomas J. Feder
BELLEVILLE, ILLINOIS

Let's Hear from an Expert

What follows is a lightly edited transcript of one of our Inside Patient Attraction™ webinars that aired in August 2016 featuring Lori Wood, SmartBox's former Director of Digital Marketing.

Lori has more than 14 years' experience in all facets of marketing. Given her bent for analytics, she emerged as an expert in Google AdWords and Google Analytics. She's developed campaigns in digital and event marketing, direct mail, and public relations.

She's someone who stays abreast of the very latest changes in search engine optimization, and there's no one better qualified to lay out what dentists need to do to be found online.

Inside Patient Attraction™ August 2016

Colin: Welcome to the August edition of Inside Patient Attraction™. I'm Colin Receveur.

Today I want to talk about why your website is worthless unless you're doing specific things to actually be seen by your prospects. Now, every marketing company out there in the world offers SEO and they tell you how great it is, but what we're going to talk about today is why all SEO was not created equal. As a dentist, you probably know that not all crowns are created equal, right? There's the $500 crown and the $1,000 crown and the $1,500 crown that you probably place somewhere in that range. All SEO was not created equal, either, and today we're going to talk about the big pitfalls and the golden things that you need to be doing to get your website found by the kinds of patients that you want to attract.

Lori, welcome on the show.

Lori: Thank you. Thanks for having me.

Colin: Thank you. Today I want to talk about a very important topic for dentists, and that's SEO, or search engine optimization. A lot of dentists think they're getting SEO, they're doing SEO, they're getting all these things, but are you really doing the right things to attract new patients? That's going to be what we're going to talk about today, is what are these specific things that you need to be doing to attract more and better patients? Lori, tell me. Let's start off with the most basic right now. Why is a dentist interested in SEO?

Lori: Well, search engine optimization, or SEO, is a huge part of anything digital marketing. If you have a website, you have to do some SEO to make sure that you can show up. There's a lot to it. There are a lot of moving parts. There are a lot of things on the back end that people that don't specialize in this type of services, they don't know what to do. So, having a digital marketer be able to kind of pave the landscape for what they're going to do with SEO, it's huge because it's constantly changing. It's a constantly changing environment and it's something that even we don't know, so parts of it are really, really gray. You have to stay up on the industry and be able to really know what's going on.

Colin: From a consumer's perspective, why does a dentist want to do SEO?

Lori: Now, any one person of the people that are on the internet and they're looking for something, a specific service or anything that they're looking to buy, they start on the internet; if you're not able to show up on that first page, 75 percent of those users, if they can't find you on the first page, then you're lost to them, so that's a really big thing. You have to be able to show up on that first page.

Colin: They don't go to the Yellow Pages anymore?

Lori: Not anymore.

Colin: I thought they went through the Yellow Pages.

Lori: The internet has taken over.

Colin: Yeah. The Yellow Pages have gone by the wayside.

Lori: Right. You know what, though? To be honest, people do go to yellowpages.com sometimes, but they still find you on the internet.

Colin: True.

Lori: Right.

Colin: What would you consider ... You see not only SEO plans that we put together, but some competitive SEO plans. What would you say would be things to look for that might be what we'll call gray area in the SEO world? What are things that some SEO companies might put in there, but don't necessarily do anything for the dentist?

Lori: Really, the big thing about SEO and anything when it comes to digital marketing is that you're competing against everyone. The big thing about it is that the digital landscape is huge. There's lots of people that are all competing for that same piece of the pie, so not only are our dentists competing against one another in small towns, but they're also competing against all the big-box companies that have huge marketing dollars and are able to spend their money in other areas. To be able to show up organically, SEO-wise, and to know all of these backend pieces that are constantly moving and keep your website at the very top, it's huge.

It's a big task, and someone really has to know what to do. There's lots of things like link building and keywords and a lot of things on the backend that most people wouldn't know. I think it's very easy for someone to come in that's in the advertising industry and say, "Hey. You need to do this, this, and this," but there are some very specific things for our dentists, I think, that SmartBox really has a handle on that other companies may not.

Colin: Tell me about some of those things you mentioned like link building, backlinks. What are those?

Lori: Link building, it's a concept, a practice that SEO marketers such as myself use in order to pull links into the website. What that does for Google and the other SERPs is it shows them the authority for that page, and if you have lots of backlinks and lots of people wanting to link to the content on your page, it shows Google you have authority in the industry. For a company such as us that does content writing, blog posting, that sort of thing, obviously we're very up-to-date when it comes to the world of dentistry, so we're able to create content, build backlinks to the most appropriate directories that have to do with that service, so it shows Google that we have lots of authority – that website really knows what they're doing and that they're a top player in that – which will show at the top of the SERPs.

Colin: Lori, tell me about duplicate content and penalties. What can you do to get Google mad at you?

Lori: There's lots of things you can do to make Google mad at you. Google holds about 80 to 90 percent of the market share when it comes to search engines, so of course when you're familiar with Yahoo and Bing and some of the other search engines, Google is really the king. Of those, all the people that searched with Google, 80 to 90 percent of them, Google is really the master at these algorithms that determine whether or not a website is going to show up at the very top of the search engine rankings. There are a lot of things specifically with the newest algorithm, Penguin, that have really been geared towards websites that have bought backlinks.

A couple of years ago, as SEO has really taken off and become a really, really big thing, years ago, in the last couple of years what's happened is that Google is on to some of these black hat tactics that SEO marketers use such as link building, keyword stuffing, which I'm sure we'll probably talk about here in a little bit. There's lots of other things out there, but there's some really big ones that you can make Google mad at you, and you can fall off the ranks and you'll never get it back no matter how good your SEO is. Backlink buying and keyword stuffing are the big ones.

Duplicate content though – content is certainly, per the term "content is king," that's a biggie in the SEO world. The content that you write for your site lets Google know what that site is about. It gives them a really good idea of how to crawl that site and what to show when people put a keyword term into a search engine.

When you have duplicate content, it's confusing to Google and the crawlers and the bots, so if you have a website and you're Smart-Box for dental marketing, and there's another website out there that's similar, it would be very easy for that other website to steal your content off of your website, but Google knows. Google knows and they can look at it and say who has the unique, relevant content, when was it first published, and that's how Google determines whether or not it is a duplicate content strike against you.

The algorithms really do not like duplicate content because it's so easy for people to steal information on the web, and so Google created the algorithms to say, "Nope. This is unique and if it's unique, then you get the credit for it."

Colin: So Google, if I remember right, they actually introduced talking about backlink buying. They actually introduced a disavow link tool.

Lori: They did, yes.

Colin: For actually disavowing links that maybe somebody else is trying to use to sabotage your website with.

Lori: Yeah.

Colin: How does that work?

Lori: This is a tool that is found in Webmaster Tools and that's an area that the digital marketing team here at SmartBox is very, very familiar with, is Webmaster Tools. We look at a lot of things within Webmaster Tools to make sure that the site is working accurately and that all of the links are redirected properly and the site is loading the proper way. There's lots of things that we look at on the backend to make sure that Google is really interested in, but the backlinks tool is something that we use to make sure that no one is sabotaging the websites. That's something that can happen a lot when it comes to backlinks.

There are a lot of ways on the internet for competitors to really hurt your website. They can create faulty backlinks that have nothing to do with your site, that really test Google's what they call authority to your site. It could be spam. They could put spam links on your site. There are a lot of companies out there that use backlink-buying tools and they'll purchase a lot of backlinks to a website because there used to be an idea in the world of marketing that the more backlinks you had at the site, obviously the better your site is, and so there were agencies that came up several years back and said, "Hey. If you want to buy a lot of links to your website and really show Google, and raise your organic search value, then you can do that by purchasing backlinks."

With the new algorithms, with Penguin, all of that changed, and so there's a tool now with Webmaster Tools that allows you to disconnect some of those links in case someone is sabotaging your website, in case they're doing unnecessary backlinks or any way that they're trying to make your website look bad in the eyes of Google. There's ways to clean that up a little bit.

Colin: Let's talk about, generally, what is all this SEO stuff? The crawlers and the page rank. Tell me about how all this works together.

Lori: Okay. When it comes to the crawlers, most of the time when I speak of search engines for the sake of being able to give most of the merit to Google because Google does hold 80 to 90 percent of the people that are searching on the internet, but the search engines, we call them SERPs in our world, it's the search engines. What they do is they go on to a site, and they have something that they call spiders and crawlers and bots that go on to the site. They crawl the website to find out exactly what your website is about.

Their crawlers go in. They look for specific keywords, look for certain tags, look for certain categories, certain things within your website that show them what that site is about, so then a user like yourself goes in and searches for a dentist within New Albany, Indiana, Google knows exactly which sites to portray to the user.

The crawlers and the bots, there's lots of things that they look for. One thing that's really interesting and what's unique about search engine marketing, and anything digital marketing really, but search engine marketing specifically, is that it's a really gray area. Not a lot of people know. There's not hard, fast rules when it comes to SEO. You have to really be up on the industry. You have to really follow the trends. You have to really do a lot of testing on your own to find out what's working.

That's one thing here at SmartBox, between all the people that are on my team, they have a lot of industry experience. We've done a lot of research. We've gone through a lot of training to learn what we've done and we keep up-to-date on all of the things that are happening in the industry to make sure that we're abreast of everything that's happening because the algorithms change so fast.

Between our experience and knowing how the dental industry works, we've been able to find out, "Hey, what's really, really going to work for our dentists, and what are these crawlers and these bots and all of these guys looking for when it comes to dentistry?" So I think we've got a pretty good handle on how that works now.

Colin: Let's start with the basic layer, if you want to call it. That is, what you need to do on your website to do SEO – quote, unquote – right?

Lori: To do SEO, right.

Colin: What needs to be looked at on your actual website to not only do the initial SEO but ongoing, to make sure that you're looked at with a preferred light from Google?

Lori: I think you hit the nail on the head when you said the start of SEO and then the ongoing SEO because SEO is something that is ongoing. It's not something that happens just, it's one and done, you launch your website, and you're finished. Really, the big things to think about when it comes to ... As of 2016, the biggies are to make sure that you have a mobile website. Google wants to make sure that it's a level playing field for anyone that's searching on the internet, so they want to make sure that if you have a mobile device or even an iPad, or if you have a computer or what have you, however you're choosing to search, that everyone has an ability to do so, so a mobile responsive website is of great importance.

You have to make sure that your website has very clean content when it comes to what you're talking about, so our dentists want to make sure that their website is specifically about dentistry and maybe not about dentistry and waffles. It has to make sure that it's all about dentistry. There needs to be very clean, concise images within the website.

There's a lot of things on the backend that we do called image optimization. We make sure that all of the meta descriptions, which are fancy words, and all of the tags are optimized, the website is optimized specifically for the services that are being offered. The website has to have a nice, clean sitemap so that when those crawlers crawl that website, they can easily find what they're looking for on the website.

Colin: Sitemap is kind of like a roadmap for your website?

Lori: Correct. It tells the Google bots how to get to where they need to go on the website, so it's, like you said, it's a nice roadmap of what's going on within that site.

Colin: Cool. What needs to be done on an ongoing basis with the website to get it ranked higher?

Lori: When it comes to ongoing SEO, the key for a website to really perform the way that it should on the internet is fresh and unique and relevant content that's constantly being added to that site. The way that Google looks at it is that if you have a website and you're constantly adding blogs or updating pictures or tweaking the content on that page based on the behavior of your users, Google looks at you and says, "Okay. This is someone that's really maintaining your website, and I know that you're current and I know that you're doing everything that you need to do, so you're going to get some props in my book for that," and it'll raise your rankings a little bit.

That ongoing optimization is something that my team, for instance, goes in and makes sure that all the images look great so that if someone were to go to Google and type in "porcelain veneers," the next thing that would come up would be an image that's optimized for porcelain veneers, meaning that whoever is looking for it is going to see exactly what they're looking for portrayed in those images.

There's a lot of things on the backend. There's a lot of code cleanup. There's a lot of things we do within Webmaster Tools to make sure that the site is loading properly, like we talked about a little bit earlier.

Google looks at that as a site that's being well-maintained, as a site that is just that. It's well-maintained and it's one that really deserves a little bit more of a raise in the ranks than one that's not.

Colin: How important is site speed these days? You mentioned load times and whatnot. How does that play into the whole picture?

Lori: No one has any patience anymore, right? When we go to a website, we want it up just like that. We want to be able to see it. We don't want one that we click on a image and the image takes forever to load. What happens? You get mad and you leave the site and you'll go somewhere else, right? The key is, Google really wants your site to load within four to five seconds, so you want to make sure that all the pages within your site, the images can load really nice and really quickly, and that the content comes up quickly and that someone can look through it very quickly because if not, it's something that we call the user could "bounce," which means they're going to bounce off the site and go somewhere else.

Colin: To the next dentist down the road.

Lori: To the next dentist down the road, right.

Colin: On the website, what kind of things do you want to see for interactivity or what kind of things can lead to a negative user experience and negative SEO?

Lori: Google is all about user experience. Google wants to make sure that when someone comes to the site, it's easy for them to navigate, easy for them to get around, easy to make sure they can get what they're looking for. Some of the things that can get in the way are bad links, links within the site that don't work, that are broken or maybe linked to nowhere or linked to something completely off-topic. Some other things are sometimes people can get carried away with the ads that they have on their website or any kind of blinking kind of gimmicky type of ...

Colin: Distractions.

Lori: ... giveaways. Right, distractions. Google definitely looks at that when it comes to user experience. A big thing is really, it's interactive. Everyone likes to be able to take quizzes or they know to be able to click on something and get something in return, so a big thing for Google recently has been any kind of user experience when it comes to something that's interactive on the website. That typically is something that users really enjoy and that it keeps them around the website a little bit longer, and so all of those things tie into the user experience piece.

Colin: The big thing from the past as well as now is keywords and keyword phrases as it's called now. How important are keywords still in today's world for our dentists?

Lori: Keywords are likely the most important piece of the whole puzzle. There's a lot of research that goes into determining what type of keyword a specific user looks for, so there's a lot of behavior, a lot of psychology that marketers look at to find out what people are looking for on the internet in order to make sure the site is optimized for that specific keyword. For instance, our dentists, we spend a lot of time doing a lot of keyword research to determine how are all the different ways people go into a search engine and how they type in. What do they type in in order to find that website? Do they look for dentists in their city? Do they search by zip codes? Do they look for specific services?

There's lots of different variables to it. It's funny. What we found is that it's very different depending on what region people live in, what specifically a dentist might specialize in or if it's general dentistry. It really just depends on … There's a lot of things that go into it. I think the takeaway is that there's a lot of research that goes into finding exactly what people are looking for on the internet. You also have to have the right tools to know what happens to someone when they do search something on the internet and then what happens when they go to site.

Is there a specific pattern? Is it, cosmetic dentistry leads to teeth whitening, and then on to something else, or is it they're specifically going into the internet and looking for teeth whitening? There's a lot of things on the backend that we look at to see, What is it? What's the behavior there? What are the keywords? What are they looking for? To top it off is that it's not just about the keyword, not just about finding what they're looking for, but then Google comes around and gives us some rules that say, "Well, I want you to talk about that specific keyword, but I don't want you to talk about it too much because if you talk about it too much, I'm going to ding you within the algorithm."

So there's a very fine line and there's no hard, fast rules into how many keywords on a page are too many keywords. I think the key there is to make things seem natural so that a user that comes to the site, a visitor comes to the site, they make sure that when they're reading the content it's not overwhelming to them, so keywords are a complicated thing. There's a fine line to how people search and how much is too much on a website, but it's definitely the main part of SEO. Everything revolves around that keyword.

Colin: Pulling all this stuff that you need to be doing for SEO together, how much of your time and your team's time do you spend, let's say, on a typical Elite client of ours? How much time on a monthly basis from you and your entire team goes into one elite client doing search engine optimization?

Lori: Oh, gosh. That's a full-time job. In order to compete with digital space on the internet, it takes a hand in it all of the time, not to mention the actual tasks that we're handling on a day-to-day basis. There's the content writing and the image optimization and all of the social media piece of it and the blog writing, the keyword research, and all of that good stuff. There's a whole list of tasks that we do to make sure that the sites stay high organically, but there's an awful lot of research that we do in the background, in the back-end too, to make sure that we know what's going on in the industry, so it's not just about the dentists, but it's also about Google and what's Google doing, what's changing, what's happening within the industry?

So it's a continuous education. It's a continuous education for our team and then it's also testing and experimenting and finding out what's working, so it's definitely a full-time job for one person for one client. We have an entire team dedicated to our clients.

Colin: What about, when you're pulling all this together? Give me a high-level overview of what one of our SEO packages looks like; what you're doing, where you're spending your time on that monthly basis.

Lori: Sure. My team, our head is stuck in analytics all the time. We're looking to find out what it is that brings someone to a website – What's the behavior that they take on the website? Where do they go from one page to the next? We're looking to find out how much time they're spending. At what point are we losing or are we not losing visitors during a specific time? Because eventually people, they're not going to spend 15 minutes on a website. They're going to move their way around to find what they're looking for, and then pick up the phone and call our dentists. That's the hope.

Colin: Oh, yeah.

Lori: Our SEO packages revolve around those analytics. The first couple of months we really learn a lot about the behavior of the users and then we're constantly tweaking at that point forward to make sure that we're getting as many calls as we can. Our SEO packages, what do they look like? They look like a lot of research in regards to keywords, building the sites to make sure that they're up to Google standards, making sure that the website is optimized for those keywords and for those services that we're looking for, and then an ongoing effort to make sure that all the webmaster checks come out right, all the mechanics of the website are correct, all the coding on the website is correct, all the fancy stuff on the backend that probably no one can read and understand except for myself.

Then all of the things that ... the trends within the industry, so the packages, it's broad and it's ongoing. Sometimes it's not as black and white as one might want to be able to see it because there are so many moving parts to it.

Colin: Some of the buzzwords in the industry that I've heard lately are behavioral marketing and neurolinguistic programing and evidence-based marketing. Would you say that those are pieces ...

Lori: Absolutely.

Colin: It kind of sounds like you're talking about those things without using those words.

Lori: Right. Everyone searches differently. Different generations search differently. They're looking for specific different things that are going to fulfill their own needs, so we have to look at some things. For instance, we may market Invisalign to someone very, very different than we might market traditional metal braces to someone else.

We do a lot of communication. There's a lot of communication that happens with our dentists to make sure, who is your perfect target audience? What's that persona look like? How can we make sure that the website is modeled after that persona to attract that persona?

There's lots of things that go into it, so when it comes to the website design, there's that piece of it, but then there's also, how can I speak in the right tone and the right voice to the right person to make sure that I attract them, get them to come to the site, stick around long enough, but then ultimately get them to make a phone call? So absolutely, there's a lot of behavioral marketing that goes into it. The SEO piece of it is a piece of that because we have a whole group of writers that write to that persona, and then we optimize for that persona. Lots of moving parts.

Colin: Yeah. For the dentist that wants to do the SEO himself, that wants to maybe hire a staff member that does the SEO, what advice can you give to that dentist?

Lori: I think that a lot of people would be able to go to the internet and probably find enough research on the internet because it's such a widely talked-about topic in terms of SEO. They could find what they need in order to probably do it themselves or maybe enlist a co-worker to do it for them. The bottom line is that doing SEO is not what makes dentists money. Being a dentist is what makes dentists money, so they don't want to spend their time doing SEO. They want to have someone who knows what they're doing, who can do the research for them, and stay on top of the industry, do it for them, otherwise it's really money down the drain for them.

Colin: What do you see as our niche in the dental market? I mean, how important is it to have an SEO company that does only dentists versus any SEO company out there in the world?

Lori: Right. I do hear that quite often. There's a lot of talk in the industry about, SEO is SEO; it doesn't matter who you're doing SEO for. It's certainly not true. We talked a little bit about the behavior of the users that go to the website and what people are looking for. Being able to provide SEO services for a niche market, it's an amazing opportunity for our dentists to rise to the top of those ranks and get more patients because there's someone on the backend, our SmartBox digital marketing team, that are looking specifically for them and looking for their patients on their behalf on the internet, and enticing them to come to our website.

The most unique portion about what SmartBox can offer when it comes to SEO and digital marketing is that we're really trying to elicit a very atypical response when it comes to digital marketing than just getting a web response on the internet. A lot of digital agencies out there, they look at that as a success. Let's submit a contact form, and that's as far as it goes. What we're really trying to do is get phone calls to that office and in order to get phone calls to that office, we know what works, we know what we can put on a website that would entice someone to pick up their phone and call rather than looking around the internet, submitting a form, or trying to schedule online. I think that's really the difference for us, is that we know what's going to get someone to pick up the phone, and how that office can get them in their chair and then in turn sell them.

Colin: Talking about phone calls, how are you tracking the results from the SEO and the marketing that you and your team are doing?

Lori: We tagged all of the phone numbers that come in so we know exactly where the traffic is coming from. We can see if it's coming from an AdWord that we're using when it comes to Google AdWords, or we can see if it's an organic search result. There's lots of different things that we can see on the backend.

Then we have a team that listens to every call. We can tell exactly where they're calling from. Are they our new patient? We also want to look to find out how many of those calls are actually getting scheduled, and that's a big thing for us. We can take all the information, and slice it and dice it any way that we want to, and find out exactly where they're coming from, but ultimately it comes from the number of phone calls that are coming into the office, and how many patients that are getting scheduled.

Colin: We specialize in helping dentists that want more patients, more profits, and ultimately more freedom from the dental practice. If that sounds like you, if you're a dentist that's interested in doubling or tripling your practice, give one of our practice consultants a call. They'll do a market analysis, a practice blueprint for your particular practice, your particular situation that can show you the path to attracting more and better patients. Well, thanks for being on the show, Lori.

Lori: Thanks for having me.

Colin: I appreciate your time. Thanks for viewing and hanging out. Thanks for giving us your time to learn about what you need to grow your practice, and attract more and better patients. We appreciate it very much and we look forward to bringing you another edition of Inside Patient Attraction™ next month. Keep moving forward.

SEO Doesn't Make You Any Money

Your website and the rest of your online marketing definitely need ongoing, state-of-the-art search engine optimization to ensure that your practice is found on organic search. But the key word there is "ongoing." At least some of your competitors are paying someone to keep their SEO current. In the meantime, those dentists are making money. This is one area where dentists are best served by outsourcing their SEO to a company that specializes in the unique needs of dental practices.

If you don't believe that it's worth it to pay someone to do something you could conceivably do yourself, let me ask you this: do you really believe that replacing the shingles on your building yourself is a good use of your time? Is that why you went to dental school?

Of course not. You went to dental school to learn how to solve people's dental problems. You went to dental school to change lives and to make a good living while doing that. You belong with your patients, not taking a flyer on highly technical things that you can have done well for the cost of one or two new dental patients.

Besides, your hourly rate is almost certainly much higher than a roofer's. Pay someone less to do your SEO than what you'll earn by seeing patients in the time you'll save.

That's one of the things that I found with my old website – we did it, and it was great, and it was inexpensive, and two years later it wasn't anything. It was just there.

I didn't realize how much needs to go into a website all the time, and it's just too much for somebody to do who owns a small business.

– Dr. Sean M. Hanson
SALEM, OREGON

Getting Found Is Just the Start of the Battle

Dentists who take the required SEO steps to be certain that their prospects find them online compete on at least a level playing field against their competition. Placing high in organic search engine results also confers a certain credibility that your prospects may find attractive.

However, a single visit to your website, blog, or social media page may not be enough to convince your prospects that you could be **the** dentist for them.

The Second Pillar, Conversion, is where that happens.

Survival Strategies

1. Advertising is hit-or-miss. A Patient Attraction System™ works 24/7 to attract more and better patients.

2. If you're not on the first page of Google search results, forget it.

3. Getting found online takes top-notch SEO, excellent website design, quality content as defined by Google, and a lot more.

4. All of those are **very** labor-intensive, and you won't make any money doing any of them yourself.

5. Your website is the linchpin of your Patient Attraction System™. Make sure it answers your prospects' questions in ways they'll understand.

6. Your website absolutely **must** be mobile-compatible.

7. "Black hat" SEO tactics fail and may get your website banned by Google.

Our new patients are up markedly from when our website went live.

I can track back and see an extra – it started out as five or 10, now it's more like an extra 10 or 15, 20 – more new patients than we were getting prior to our agreement, or our working relationship, with SmartBox.

I know, unequivocally, that that website is attracting people and generating phone calls, and then it's our job to turn those phone calls into visits.

It's definitely working, no question about it.

– Dr. Matthew Burton
CLEARWATER, FLORIDA

7
The Second Pillar: Conversion

"Google bought YouTube for 1.65 billion dollars, which to you and I means they want more hits on YouTube videos, so they rank them higher in listings."

– Dr. Woody Oakes, President, The Profitable Dentist & Excellence in Dentistry

You may not be a fan of the old-time silent movies, but you've almost certainly seen short clips of one. The actors are on screen, overacting, and the dialogue shows up as text in a box at the bottom. The actors had to overact to convey the emotional impact of the printed dialogue.

They did have a little help, though – when those movies first ran in theaters, the soundtrack was provided by someone in the theater playing a piano!

Do you know what killed the silent film industry in this country? Adding sound to the film itself. Actually being able to *hear* the nuances of what the actors were saying during the film was an unbeatable advantage. Silent movies went the way of the dinosaurs.

There's a lesson here for dentists. Reading is one thing. Seeing and hearing is far more powerful.

The Trust Factor

Successful dentistry is based on patients liking and trusting you. That can be an uphill battle; it's uncommon for people to trust someone they haven't met or even spoken to. You need to give your dental prospects proof that you're the only logical choice to solve their dental problems.

One of the best ways for your prospects to come to know you and trust you is through online videos.

The Power of Video

Web pages with video are 53 times more likely to be seen than pages without video. That alone is reason enough for dentists to have videos on their websites and on their YouTube channels.

Your own videos give your prospects a chance to become familiar with you. You have the opportunity to share your expertise concerning dental problems and solutions. Both of those things are essential for them to begin to like you, to relate to you, and to trust you.

Video testimonials by your delighted patients constitute "social proof." In today's online world, video testimonials are a large part of the new word-of-mouth advertising. The other part consists of positive patient reviews on sites such as Healthgrades, Yelp, Zocdoc, and others. Videos, however, tend to have greater impact because being able to both see and hear your patients talk about you and your practice is more effective than simply reading words written by an unknown person.

Those are all good reasons for you to make broad use of online videos. However, like everything else, not all videos are created equal. Videos that are done well are assets in your search for new dental patients, but poorly produced videos are liabilities. In today's hypercompetitive online environment, searchers will click away from a website at the slightest provocation.

Your videos must be professional-level and portray you as both as an expert and as a person. And it's crucial that your videos convey a strong patient focus.

Who Are You Marketing To?

It might surprise you to learn that patients don't care about technique, training, or awards. They care about results, living happier and more fulfilled lives, and knowing that they'll be taken care of.

Too many dentists market to impress other dentists. They include a string of letters after their names and discuss dental procedures in-depth using highly technical and unfamiliar terms. That's a losing strategy. Few, if any, of your prospects will care enough about the details to look anything up. Most of them will go find a dentist who speaks to their needs in a way they can understand.

The idea that dentists market to impress other dentists isn't new; I've been saying it for years.

Here's a post from the SmartBox blog that appeared in June 2015. See if you recognize yourself.

Alphabet Soup Doesn't Attract New Patients

If you're one of those dentists who feels the need to put a string of letters after his name giving your credentials, you may be hurting your practice by doing so. As hard as this may be to read, potential patients just don't care about your bona fides.

That's right. They're not attracted to "alphabet soup."

Congratulations if you have achieved continuing education certifications. It takes a lot of hard work and time, and you should be proud of yourself.

But do yourself a favor and stop putting initials from each of those organizations or recognitions after your name when reaching out to potential patients. You know the only initials that matter to potential patients: D and R.

That's right, doctor.

The average person has no idea of the difference even between DDS and DMD. What makes you think any assortment of letters after your name increases your credibility?

This is a perfect example of dentists marketing for other dentists. Unless you are trying to reach all the dentists in your community to do their dental work, putting a string of letters behind your name is falling on blind eyes.

So what, you might ask, is the problem with putting them there?

The problem is that by putting them there, you *think* you are establishing credibility with patients and don't do the things that really establish credibility. So instead of advertising that you recently completed a rigorous process that will allow you to give patients the smile they've always dreamed about, you simply put "AACD" after your name.

As if patients know what AACD is or will bother to look it up!

A string of letters just isn't a substitute for focusing on your potential patients' wants and needs.

Now let's be clear: No one is saying you should not attend CE or seek advanced certifications. Quite the contrary: The more credentials you have, the more marketable you are.

But stop relying on letters after your name to tell the story of your qualifications. It's not that easy. You have to tell the *benefits* of those letters to prospective patients. How can you serve them *better* than someone without that training? *How* are you better qualified to address *their* needs?

That's what you have to answer. Otherwise, those prospective patients could choose a less-qualified dentist and not even realize it. And once they're gone, they're gone.

Here is one final thought: Some dentists seem to think that because they have LVI or any other combination of letters after their name that they are entitled to more patients than the kid who just graduated dental school down the street.

To be blunt: You may be more qualified, but you aren't entitled to any more patients. You'll get as many patients as you earn.

And if that kid down the street is out promoting himself and explaining to potential patients how his credentials benefit them while you count on a row of letters after your name to do it for you, your qualifications won't do you one bit of good.

Attitude Is Contagious

That "marketing to impress" attitude carries over into doctors' online videos. Dentists use words that are too highfalutin, they provide little to no explanation of what terms mean, and there's not enough context to help your patients understand. Any doctor who is marketing to impress other doctors is going to lose patients after they try to watch his or her videos. Why? Because those doctors aren't positioning themselves to be likeable and relatable – they're positioning themselves as just another asshole dentist who can't be bothered to explain things in plain English!

Okay, there are a few dental patients who get off on the technical aspects of dentistry. You probably have a couple of those in your practice. But you don't have enough, and you won't attract enough, to grow your practice.

If you want more new dental patients – and what doctor doesn't? – your marketing has to be about your *patients*' wants and needs. If you want to impress other dentists, do it by being wildly successful, not by making your own doctor videos into a clinical symposium. Don't be "that guy."

By the same token, your testimonial videos – not all of them, by any means, but a good number – have to speak to what your prospects *want*. And that's another area where too many dentists go wrong.

The Art of the Testimonial

Some people are looking for a dentist just for routine cleanings and checkups. Others are looking for someone to solve one or more dental problems. Some are looking for a dentist who understands dental anxiety – which, by the way, affects more than 130 million people in the U.S. to some extent – and who they can trust to take care of them.

You can convey through your videos your patient focus, your concern for patients' well-being, and the steps you take to ensure a great outcome and their comfort. That's only part of the battle, though, in convincing your prospects to choose you.

The other part, and the more credible part, is when your current patients speak on camera about the experience your future patients can expect with you and with your practice. Again, not all videos are created equal. There's an art to getting patient testimonial videos that your prospects can relate to and identify with. That art wasn't covered in your dental school curriculum.

Let Them Speak

Your patients aren't professional on-camera spokespeople, and trying to script them will come off as artificial and forced. That undermines their credibility, and credibility is absolutely crucial to producing testimonials with impact. Let them speak in their own words. However, it's fine to ask them before taping what they'd like to talk about. That may help them organize their thoughts. You'll probably need to do some probing to get more than a general endorsement of your practice.

Another important thing to anticipate is having to edit your testimonials before you put them online. "Normal" people rarely speak in complete sentences. They ramble, they repeat themselves, they go off on tangents. A coherent testimonial that tells a story has far more impact than a video that leaves viewers scratching their heads and wondering what it was actually about.

Real people saying really nice, believable things about how your efforts, and those of your staff, made their lives better – that's the "formula" for great testimonial videos. Ignore that formula at your own risk.

Your videos help your prospects view you as relatable, expert, and trustworthy. Your testimonial videos provide social proof for all your online marketing.

Once likeability, trust, and credibility are established, you and your practice become **the only logical choice** for patients' problems.

Lights, Camera ... Uh-Oh.

That covers the human side of your patient testimonials, but what about the technical side? Yes, you can shoot "hallway" videos on your iPhone – and too many dentists do – but getting high-quality results will be a fluke.

Professional-quality videos require planning to get the right, uncluttered setting. You need an area free from outside noise and not visually distracting to your patients or to viewers.

You'll also need the right equipment – good, adjustable, lighting; a good-quality camera and tripod; and either a directional microphone or a lapel mike. That's one of the problems with videos shot on smartphones: the microphones pick up *everything*, often things that neither you nor your patient were aware of. Many otherwise good testimonials have been ruined because no one was aware of the vehicle horns blaring in the background.

Planning and the right equipment – those essentials are sadly lacking in many dentists' self-produced videos.

And then you'll need a good editing system to smooth out the bumps and produce videos that will hold your viewers' attention.

If you think I'm making too much about the need for top-flight testimonial videos, think about this: If you have the choice of watching a video with great lighting and sound versus one with numerous distractions, which one are you going to choose?

And which option speaks better to your professionalism as a dentist?

The quality of video that you guys have on the sites and stuff, I really like that.

I've tried to do some of our patient testimonials, and it's not near the same quality that you have.

I think that's excellent.

– Dr. Mike Fuesting
DANVILLE, ILLINOIS

Let's Hear from an Expert

What follows is a lightly edited transcript of our April 2016 Inside Patient Attraction™ webinar. I'm joined by Alex Hall. At the time, he was our Director of Digital Storytelling and in charge of our video production department. As SmartBox has grown, he's moved on to other duties and is now our Director of Special Projects.

Alex has many years of experience in conceptualizing, directing, producing, and editing testimonial videos. In fact, he's produced more than 10,000 doctor and patient testimonials videos for SmartBox dentists! If you want to know how to create the online videos that will bring more new patients to your practice – and have them prepared to accept your case solutions – this is a must-read.

Inside Patient Attraction™ April 2016

Colin: Welcome to Inside Patient Attraction™. I'm your host, Colin Receveur. This is the April 2016 edition. I'm joined by our Director of Digital Storytelling today, Alex Hall. Thanks for being on board, Alex. We get to chat a little bit.

Alex: It's a pleasure.

Colin: We're going to chat today, and we'll to tell you about how you can attract more patients, more profits, and more freedom and how you can leverage the power of video because video, it's the social proof, it's how you can get your patients to know, like, and trust you. We're going to show you how in this edition.

We're talking today about video, but not just any video, not just the little flip cam videos that you flail around and record in your office. We're talking about leveraging the right kind of video to attract more and better patients into your practice.

If you look at the statistics, it's overwhelming. You look at the auto industry, the real estate industry. Michael Jordan had an awesome drone tour of his 30-million-dollar house that he's trying to sell if you haven't seen it and they're doing that. Drone technology is available for everybody now. All these other industries are embracing it.

I'm going to talk today with Alex about how to get dentists to embrace video.

You look at the stats, forced research. If a picture is worth a thousand words, a video is worth 1.8 million words per minute. That's the nature of communication. It's 80 percent of humans can make communications nonverbal. It's how we talk. It's gestures and posturing and tone of voice. It's Robert Cialdini.

You've heard of Cialdini?

Alex: I've heard of Cialdini every day.

Colin: It's trust, it's social proof, it's developing that bond with your patients. What do you think, Alex? You're the head of our digital storytelling team here, essentially the video and everything we do. What do you see as the compelling reasons why dentists must be leveraging video in 2016?

Alex: One of the biggest challenges that dentists have now in the digital age ... You don't have free consultations, really. Patients are really taking advantage of that, and so you have to be able to reach out and develop that trust with your patients before they come into your office, and videos are tremendous way to do that. If you can have a great video or multiple videos on your page that put your personality out there, who you are, what you represent, that lets them trust you and takes advantage of Cialdini's principles about trust and social proof – and you can put patient testimonials on there as well.

Also, you want to position yourself as the expert. Now, you can have a lot of great content on your website. You can have a lot of detailed content as far as the written word, but video is the one way you can really put yourself out there as the expert, frame yourself as a trusted source of information when it comes to dental care. By the time they walk into your office, they already trust you. They already feel like you're the person that can help them. They already feel like you are their savior for all their dental needs. Right?

Colin: Yeah. I hear so often from our dentists that the patients that they have coming in say they're pre-educated, they're pre-qualified because they already know everything about that dentist in the practice before they ever walk in the door. How can you get that level of humanization or what do you do with the video team at SmartBox to achieve the letting people get to meet the dentist before they ever walk in the door?

Alex: We try to go into doctors' offices and talk to them about what makes their practice different. What makes them special. It's a flooded market with dentists right now, and the people who can be the early adopters as far as video – or at this point, you're kind of semi-late adopters of video. The people who can embrace that and really put themselves and their ideas and their unique perspective on dentistry and patient care out there are going to be the ones who really take advantage of not only the generation that's getting older.

Everybody has got an iPhone nowadays. Everybody's tech-savvy. My grandma has an iPhone. It's scary. You don't want Grandma really having an iPhone. It's a dangerous world out there, but you'll be able to take advantage of millennials and all these people who are really tech-savvy who want to take in all that information through video and on their phone.

Colin: What do you see … One of the questions I get a lot is with the older generation, the baby boomers having all the down needs – are they getting online? If you're working with a fee-for-service practice that is targeting that older generation, how are you getting in front of them? Are they all on the internet, or do you see less of the older generation on, or what does your research say on that?

Alex: The baby boomers have embraced the internet. They are on Facebook. They use their mobiles. They use their iPads. They're all over it. One thing that's generation agnostic is people don't have time, and so whether you're trying to market to millennials or whether you're trying to market to baby boomers or an older crowd who may need dentures or whatever the service is, people don't have time. They don't have time to go through your entire website. They don't have time to do anything but get the information they need quickly.

A video that's sub-two minutes or really to-the-point video that's sub-two minutes is the way they want to ingest the information. If they can see social proof quickly, they're going to call your office. They're going to make an appointment. They're going to feel like they trust you already.

Once you get them in your chair, no longer do you have to build trust like you used to have to in the old days. You go in a dentistry in the '80s and '90s, you used to have to get the free consultation; the relationship started in the chair. Now you can have the videos do the work for you. You can build the relationship before you even meet the patient, and that is a benefit to doctors as far as trying to close drill-and-fill or big-case dentistry.

Colin: What's the importance of the social proof and the trust with dentists?

Alex: It's a very personal thing, and I think dentists know. Any dentist watching out there knows some of the biggest hurdles are fear of the dentist, fear of pain, and it's such a personal experience to have hands in your mouth, as dentists know.

Colin: Absolutely.

Alex: To build that social proof that you are not only qualified but you're gentle, you're a nice person, they can relate to you – all these things help calm patients down and make them want to come to your office. You don't have to drag people, and you don't have to do race to the bottom, free whitening, 80 percent off your service.

Colin: It's a slippery slope.

Alex: It is a slippery slope to the bottom. If you can build that social proof, people will pay for value.

Colin: One of the biggest things with video that when we work with a specialist or a large elective-case dentist is they've got to be the expert. How can video set up a dentist to actually be the experts of care in their marketplace?

Alex: If you're a dentist who does large elective-case dentistry – everybody and their brother is – it's the comfortable dentist. Basically, the "we-won't-hurt-you" dentist. Now, that's a pretty low bar. If you went to Subway and they said, "You know, we're gonna guarantee you a sandwich with bread and meat." That's …

Colin: It's pretty bad.

Alex: It's a pretty low bar. You have to be the expert. Everybody's got a guy. I got a guy who can give me a special deal on a car. I got a guy who can … if my computer system breaks down, I got an expert to go to. I know I am only going to go to that one guy. Dentists have to put themselves out there to be that guy, to be the absolute expert. When people think of dental problems, whether very, very complex, a lot of cases are very, very simple drill-and-fill, they think of that dentist's name.

The way to do that is to position yourself, set the frame of the conversation as the expert early on using your website, using social media. You can push these videos out everywhere, and you can use them in other marketing as well and it doesn't just have to be videos of the dentist himself talking. You want to have videos of your staff. You want to have videos of the atmosphere of your office.

You're basically getting the patient an overview of your office, of the atmosphere, of the feeling. These videos can be structured. It's a psychological tool.

Colin: You've touched on something there that I want to explore. You said, you talked about integrating these videos and using them in your marketing. How can you use them online or offline? Where do they get used to position these doctors in that way?

Alex: Obviously on your website, but you can also use it for landing pages. You can use them in auto responding emails to follow up with patients to just to personalize those emails. You can use them on social media and you can use them across your marketing. About the only thing you can't use them on is a direct mail card because that gets a little expensive putting a monitor on direct mail card. That's out of the realm of possibility but that's about the only place you can't. These are the epitome … If you can do a quality, if you can, quality videos, this is the epitome of a way to touch your patients. Patients you don't even know yet and to foster that relationship before they even come into the office.

Colin: I was at a doctor's office last week, and I was consulting with him and we're working on some of his marketing. He was on his website. He was showing me the videos that he has on his website. It shows how implants work and how dentures work and how you put implants in a patient's mouth. What do you think of that?

Alex: One thing you don't want to do for fearful patients is show them the thing they're fearful of. You don't want to have videos on your site that get into the technical "here's-how-we're-going-to-place-the-implant." Even though it's not scary for the dentist, you're driving away a great percentage of your potential patients. You're repelling them because they're scared of that. They have a fear and they don't want to … No one wants to see it. No one wants to know how the sausage is made. They just want to enjoy the sausage.

Colin: Good analogy. What you're telling people is for those doctors that have the clinical, the surgery videos on their website, get rid of them?

Alex: Get rid of them. They're scaring patients away, and let's be honest, no one cares about the technical skill.

Colin: How the sausage is made.

Alex: No one cares about the technical skill it takes to put that crown in, to put that implant in. All they care is they're out of pain, they are comfortable, and they can chew again.

Colin: What kind of video should they be using on their site?

Alex: Videos that highlight your practice. What you're about. Why you are the epitome of dentistry. Why they should come to you. Most people have developed a practice slogan, how you go about doing things that help serve your patients better. Putting those things out in video, putting testimonials of patients who have had a great experience. You could do it by people who just love your office. You can do it by the niches that you choose, whether it's cosmetic dentistry or whether it's implants, full-restoration dentistry.

Patients that have gone through that process and are able to tell other people, "Hey, it's not scary. It was painless. I have a million-dollar smile." Whatever that case, putting that social proof on your website just enhances your reputation in the marketplace and makes people want to come, and instead of waiting to get dentistry done, they'll be proactive about it.

Colin: What do you find when you're developing these testimonials, the social proof for dentists? What are you putting in those? What kind of questions are you asking? By the same token, what are you not asking the patients to talk about in the videos?

Alex: I'm not asking the patients to describe the procedure. I'm not asking the patients to describe anything other than the emotional context of their experience because we relate as human beings through emotion, right? We all have the Facebook app we'll hit, and it's a must-watch video and it's just an emotional, heart-wrenching video of a lion who was separated from his owner in 1976 and they reunited – everybody cries and loves that video. We relay a human level across demographics through emotions. You have to convey that emotion.

We have a great team, and so we've been able to go onsite and even have patients who will get emotionally touched in the chair and even have people cry and even have people – because it's such a personal experience going to the dentist. It can really change lives as anybody who does it knows, and capturing those stories is something that really pushes your practice above your competition.

If you want to be ... If the goal is to attract more and better patients and be a top performer in your market, this is a must-have. You have got to embrace it, and you've got to ride the wave to a better future for your practice, and video's just the way that's going to take you there.

Colin: When you're capturing these patients testimonials, how are you getting? How are you ... flat out, what are you asking? What are you asking these patients to get more than, "Yeah, it was good. It was okay. I like that dentist." How are you getting that emotional content?

Alex: I like to look at it as like mining for gold. You have to keep digging, and the way we do that is the "five whys." Why did you come to this dentist? Well, it's because my tooth hurt. Well, why did you choose us? Well, because you're the expert. Well, why? Well, I saw your commercial in there and I just thought this could be a good place for me. Why? Well, because I saw the emotional content. I saw what you've done with other patients, and I thought you could help me in. Why? Well, because my tooth has been hurting and my life has been going off the cliff.

You get these stories, but you have to dig a little bit. There's not gold lying on the surface. You don't want testimonials that just say, "What do you think about Doctor Receveur?" "He's good." Now people will do that, but you have to keep digging and you have to just ask the five whys. It's a great ... For people who want to do stuff in their own office, if you want to record testimonials in your own office, five whys. Dig a little bit, understand the emotional reason why they're there. That will serve you so much better than putting testimonials out there that are just, "He's good. He's nice. I like him." That really doesn't have that social proof that a more in-depth emotional video has.

Colin: Something that I've noticed with a lot of our clients and a lot of dentists in general are they're videoing their own testimonials. They're ... Some of them have a webcam or a flip cam. Some of them have a nice little video setup. Some of them, they don't edit them. You hear the doctor in the background asking, "How did you hear about us?" or "Why did you come here?" or "What was your experience here?"

Colin: How do you guys create compelling video, and how do you do it that's different from what the doctor can capture in his own office?

Alex: I appreciate that doctors want to capture their own testimonials because they're on the right track. They need to have those testimonials, but there is a tremendous way for having professional-quality videos. It's what people buy into. That professionalism is subconscious. The professionalism in the video is a subconscious indication to them that you are also a professional. You can't have videos that are on your flip phone and that are unedited with bad audio and then think, "Oh yeah, he's probably a great dentist too." They don't make that connection. Bad video, bad dentists. Professional video, professional dentist.

Maybe it's an unfair line to draw, but this is what you have to do to get to that professional thinking, and for patients, I think the way you show you're on that professional level is to have professional-quality video. How you do that is you have the people who come in and understand how to tell stories, because yes, there's a technical aspect to it. There's having the right gear and having the right lighting and having the right audio and having that understanding. That's one piece over here, but the real piece is understanding the psychology and the storytelling inside of the video format to be able to convey these stories.

You can do it in your office. You can pick a staff member. You can pick Susie on your staff, and Susie takes the patient into the back after they've had their root canal, whatever, and talks to them about it, and they'll probably have a big, bright window in the background and they'll say a few things and you go, "Great, I got a testimonial." Doesn't carry the same weight as something that has been professionally produced that has had intricate storytelling techniques used on it and that goes to the whole process, from the setting up of the interview and the environment to the interviewing of the person to the editing.

That's huge. The editing of what the person is saying. You see these professional testimonials, they're not just thrown up online after they're recorded. They're edited by people who really understand the psychology of storytelling and understand what people need to hear to trust that doctor. We have a team here that understands that, and so that's why our doctors are able to have that social proof out there that really helps attract more and better patients, is because those patients who haven't chosen that doctor yet feel like their needs are already addressed before they come into the office because of this high-level storytelling that takes place.

Colin: What are you seeing with doctors that capture their own videos? What are they doing wrong specifically?

Alex: Usually it's a lighting and sound issue. We all have a camera in our pocket, the iPhone. That will do a decent job. That will give you a pretty darn good image, but the audio sucks and there's no lighting and there's that level of storytelling there that isn't apparent in doctors that's doing their own videos. You could have your son-in-law do your videos, and he probably went to school for it and he could probably set up the camera and set up and gets you a decent lighting setup, but it's really – I'll go back to the psychology. It's really understanding the psychology of potential patients and what they're looking for and what will help close your deals…. Imagine having an office, imagine having a practice where patients came in already ready to accept treatment before the consultation.

Colin: Awesome.

Alex: That's easy for the dentist to be able to come in and say, "They're already ready to go." They are already ready to accept your treatment. Already, you're the expert. It takes the work out of it by putting in work and investing in your testimonial videos and getting a high-quality product at a very refined level of storytelling. You are now getting patients who are ready to accept treatment immediately walking in. How easy is that for your staff? How easy is that for you? You can really just get to the business of dentistry rather than having to sell, and I know dentists hate selling, and this takes that out of it.

Colin: Awesome. What kind of time when you're taking one of your teams out to one of our dentist clients, how much prep time is there before we get there? How much editing are you doing after you leave there? Tell me about how much time is involved with the whole production process.

Alex: We do a lot of pre-production. We plan out what we're going to do at a doctor's office, what will work best for them. We collaborate with the office to see what types of testimonials are coming in, whether they're for a big-case elective, because you have to know that in order to understand how you're going to approach the interviewing process. Once we do that, we go to the doctor's office; we make it as easy as possible. We travel with the amount of equipment and people that lets us get the job done at a high level. It's minimally invasive.

We take a nice corner of the doctor's office, film these patients coming in for one, two, three days depending on how much of a testimonial presence they want on their website, and then we come back and we spend anywhere from one to two weeks editing it and really delving into all the footage. A lot of stuff ends up on the cutting room floor because it's just not as compelling as we want it to be. Only the best of the best stuff gets to those final testimonials and ends up in the marketing system that the doctor has in order to attract those patients.

Colin: Awesome, awesome. Robert Cialdini, Dr. Robert Cialdini. We are all both very familiar with him.

Alex: *Influence*.

Colin: Yeah, *Influence*. Amazing book. If you don't know the book, go onto Amazon, it's like eight bucks. *Influence* by Robert Cialdini. The man spends his whole life figuring out how to make people do what he wants them to do. To put it into maybe crude terms, but his whole business is around convincing people to choose a favorable choice for him in a business situation. What have you seen with videos and specifically the relatability and the influence of videos to a person that's making a decision to spend $10,000, $20,000, $50,000 in their mouth?

Alex: Cialdini's principle of relatability in chatting is something we reference a lot here in that post-production, designing these testimonial type videos. The principle of relatability basically says you need to talk to people in the language they're already speaking. The conversation they're already having. You can talk to patients about amalgam versus composite fillings. You can talk to them about all the technical aspects of dentistry, but you really need to speak to them at the level that they're at and they understand. They're at an emotional state to where they're either scared of the dentist or there's some kind of wall in the way for them to come into your practice. You have to speak to them at that level. Tell them how dentistry isn't painful anymore.

This is not the dentistry of the baby boomers, where there were some bad experiences. This is ... Dentistry is pretty much painless now, and it's an improving-your-life type service. If you're speaking to them at that level and talking to them about what they're concerned about, you'll really have much better success if you're talking above their head about stuff that really people only care about when you're in CE or in dental school.

Colin: What other ways ... You've got the videos, you've produced the videos, you've got great killer emotional content, they're professionally done, they're edited, they're on your website, they're in your marketing. What other ways can you leverage video to get yourself or your video seen out there?

Alex: On your website is one of the biggest ones because that is your digital presence. It's the epicenter of your digital presence. We already know that websites and video are 53 times more likely to be seen by Google.

Colin: Who says that?

Alex: Forrester Research.

Colin: Really? Fifty-three times more likely that your website's going to be found online if you have video on your site. It's amazing. SEO with video is something that I know it's not on YouTube, the digital storytelling side, but we've got an amazing SEO team here that does optimization across the board, including video and getting videos found online. Google's putting videos right there at the top of the search engines. It's something that you can claim another spot on the search engine with great optimized video putting them on your website.

Like you said, it makes your website ... Google wants great multimedia websites that have great content and provide a great user experience, and if your website is doing that, if it's providing the right message with the right kind of video when people are staying, then they're also coming to your office and they're paying and referring, and that's what you want. It's patients that are going to pay, stay, and refer the right kinds of patients to grow your practice.

Alex: A Cisco study said by 2018 that 86 percent of all consumer internet traffic will be video, and that's huge.

Colin: It's amazing.

Alex: You can either choose to be a top performer as a dentist and get out in front of that curve and try to be out there and try to have a social proof on your website, or you can still try to be the Yellow Page guy who thinks billboards and Yellow Pages are going to get you these new wave of patients, which I think is a misnomer.

Colin: I think Yellow Pages ... I'm waiting for it to appear in the news somewhere that somebody is actually, like, writing the Yellow Pages a ticket for littering when they drop their books off everywhere because I know for me, they go straight from the outside my door into the garbage. It's a litter problem. It's not a matter of what it is. It's just trash. Straight into the garbage.

Alex: Exactly.

Colin: We've covered all kinds of awesome content here. We've talked about how to create compelling video that has emotional connections, Cialdini's social proof with patients, with staff, with your office. We've talked about how to leverage it to get 53 times the visibility. We've talked about what not to do, which maybe is the most important of all because everybody knows if they're not supposed to. We all know you're doing something wrong if you're over the speed limit. You know you're in the wrong.

We've covered how to ask patients and how to build the testimonials and how to really dive deep into finding out that conversation that the patients are already having. I appreciate you being on the show.

Alex: It's been a pleasure.

Colin: It's been awesome having you here. You have to stop back by again sometime.

Alex: All the time.

Colin: Those doctors that are interested in how they can leverage video to attract more and better patients really focus in on attracting the patients that you want into your practice, whether that's elective or large-case, fee-for-service implants and Invisalign, dentures. Whatever your niche is, your profit center, give one of our senior practice consultants a call. They'd love to talk to you. I'd love to work with you and help you out attracting more and better patients into your practice.

Tune in again for another edition of Inside Patient Attraction™, but until then, always keep moving forward.

Last month my partner and I went down to Louisville, where we did our green screen videos for our web page and had a wonderful experience.

All the prep work and time that has gone in for us to do our office work, as well as our doctor prep work, has been done by Colin and his team, and we couldn't be happier.

– Randy Schmidt
DDS, MSD, CHICAGO

Yes, You Can, but Should You?

You've read what goes into making professional-quality doctor and testimonial videos that will help attract more and better dental patients to your practice.

If you've always dreamed of being "in pictures," this might be fun for you to learn and to perfect your craft. But is it really the best use of your time and talents? As Alex pointed out, there's not just the interview and taping portion; there's also the editing. That will require you to learn a new program well enough to use it comfortably and quickly. Even after you're familiar with the editing system, you can expect to spend as much or more time editing videos as it took to shoot them.

And while you're hunched in front of a computer monitor, you're not seeing patients and making money. You're not spending time with family or friends. You're not recharging your batteries for the next working day.

There are times when it's best to outsource to experts. For almost all dentists, video is best handled by a company that understands dentistry intimately and has proven capabilities.

Managing Your Online Reputation

Videos aren't the only factor in converting new dental prospects, just the most important one.

Your prospects will also check out patient reviews from online rating sites – Yelp, Healthgrades, and even Facebook. You can control the video testimonials you put online, but the independent review sites are another animal entirely.

Your online reputation is critical to your success, and you can't afford to ignore negative reviews. With that in mind, here's a SmartBox blog post from February 2017 that will tell you how to deal effectively with unhappy patients who air their grievances online.

Is the New Word-of-Mouth Advertising Killing Your Dental Practice?

How often do you get new dental patients from your Yellow Pages ad?

The traditional means of dental marketing – YP ads, newspaper ads, and postcard campaigns – just won't cut it in today's wired (and wireless) world.

The overwhelming majority of dental prospects are looking for a dentist **online**. In part, that's due to the convenience offered by mobile search. More importantly, online has taken over because it offers access to far more information about you and your practice than has ever been possible before. Your prospects are (hopefully) perusing your website, possibly reading some of your blogs, and checking you out on Facebook or Twitter.

Most importantly, they're reading your online reviews and watching your patient testimonials. **Those** are the new word-of-mouth advertising, and dentists today largely live or die by the quality of that advertising.

A Question of Fractions

Most online review sites have a five-star rating system. Your "star" rating is usually the first thing your prospects see when they check out your reviews. Depending on how many reviews about you are posted, your score may be very robust. That means that one or two unfavorable reviews won't do much to change a rating that's based on hundreds of review.

But if you have only 20 or 30 online reviews, two or three negative reviews will do very bad things to your star rating.

Think about your dental prospects: If they see that your rating is 4.1, and your competitors' ratings are hovering around 4.7 to 4.8, who do you think they'll choose? That fraction-of-a-point difference can well make the difference between your practice's success and ultimate failure.

Think LIKE Your Prospects

A slight difference in online rating might seem like a stupid way to choose a dentist. After all, training, experience, knowledge, and the results you can deliver should weigh more heavily, right?

Wrong.

Your dental prospects don't know dentistry. They can't tell the difference between someone who has studied with industry leaders and someone who is very competent but doesn't have the credibility of attending the Spear Institute or the Malo Clinic Lisbon. They don't know dentistry, but they **do know** what they want, and that's a dentist they can **trust and relate to.**

That's why online reviews are so important to your success.

Getting 5-Star Reviews

Very few of your dental prospects and patients are strictly results-oriented. Today's dental patient is looking at the totality of the experience:

- Your online presence
- Your reviews
- The prospect's initial contact with your practice
- The prospect's comfort level in, and with, your office and dental staff
- His or her comfort level with you
- And finally, the result.

You and your practice have the opportunity to raise or lower your "rating" with every patient you come in contact with. Smart dentists will look to their policies, their procedures, and each member of their staff to make each interaction with patients the best that it can be.

The new word-of-mouth advertising can make or break your dental practice. If you've not already done so, put renewed emphasis on the patient experience. You can be sure that your competitors are.

Moving On

Providing your prospects with social proof that you're the right choice for them is essential to converting them to new patients. But that conversion is a process, not an event. To get them to pick up the phone and book an appointment, you have to stay in front of them until they're ready.

The Third Pillar, Follow-up, is how you do that.

Survival Strategies

1 Successful dentistry is based on patients liking and trusting you.

2 Prospects won't take your word for it. You have to give them "social proof."

3 Doctor and patient testimonial videos, done well, are an excellent form of social proof. Poorly done videos are liabilities.

4 You didn't go to dental school to learn to direct, shoot, and edit videos. Outsource them to a reliable company that "gets" dentistry.

5 Online videos and ratings sites are the new word-of-mouth advertising. Managing your online reputation is crucial to your success.

6 Once likeability, trust, and credibility are established, your practice becomes the only logical choice to solve patients' dental problems.

I think SmartBox has done a great job of generating phone calls to the practice, no question about that.

I think the video and photo is cutting edge, and it was cutting edge 18 months ago, and still, there's not many of my colleagues doing that.

– Dr. Matthew Burton
CLEARWATER, FLORIDA

8
THE THIRD PILLAR: FOLLOW-UP

Did you ever hear the story about the reporter who was interviewing a couple who'd been married for 65 years?

The reporter asked, "How did you two come to be married?"

The husband looked fondly at his wife and answered, "I chased her until she caught me."

If there's a moral to the story, it's in two parts – persistence pays off, and decision making is a process, not an event.

According to a study by Google, people consult an average of 10.4 sources of information before they make a buying decision. Your dental prospects go through the same process when choosing a dentist.

You saw in Chapter 7 that your online videos and patient testimonial videos can help convert browsers into converts – people who are interested in you and the services you can provide. That doesn't mean your prospects are ready to choose you.

People with a dental emergency may make a quick decision about finding a dentist to relieve their suffering. Others, without that sense of urgency, are more likely to take their time and look around. Those dental "shoppers" are 90 to 95 percent of your website visitors.

They need more information before they're willing to make a decision. You have to stay in front of them by providing that information until they're ready to choose you.

You gain a number of advantages by following up with your prospects. It might surprise you to learn that most dentists do no follow-up at all with their website visitors. The odds are overwhelming that most of those visitors – potential new patients – will be lost to the dentists.

You can't afford to let that happen.

Staying in contact with your prospects allows you to nurture and maintain the relationship. In turn, that enables you to influence them until they're ready to book an appointment.

Clearly, not every visitor to your website is a legitimate prospect **right now**. Some are "just browsing." You have to give them something in exchange for their agreement to receive further communications from you.

Reeling Them In

Offering website giveaways such as a white paper, patient newsletter, a book authored by you (or ghostwritten by a professional), or other helpful content gets you prospects' names and email addresses. That allows you to continue sending them useful information and to stay in front of them until they're ready to choose you.

But each of the patient segments you want to attract has specific interests and needs. For instance, a lot of seniors might be very interested in dental implants, but most 20-somethings won't care.

People just starting out in their careers might not have the means to afford cosmetic dentistry, but teeth whitening might be a big draw. Established professionals, on the other hand, might turn to more extensive cosmetic dentistry to enhance their professional success.

And then there are the prospects who need gum disease treatment, orthodontia, full-mouth reconstruction, and on and on.

Each of those segments requires email campaigns, text messages, and multiple other forms of contact.

Creating separate streams of content for each segment is a monumental undertaking. Arguably, it's not a good use of your time and energy. Still, that content has to be created and kept fresh if you're going to succeed in staying in front of your prospects. You could do it yourself, but is that really the best use of your time?

Creating content for your various prospect streams is a time-consuming process that demands commitment, the ability to understand and embrace your patients' mindset, and a certain level of writing skill. As with creating compelling testimonial videos, there's an art to telling your story in such a way as to motivate a prospect to pick up the phone and book an appointment. It's a different proposition than academic writing, and most dentists find it difficult to pull off. Just like doing SEO and shooting videos, you didn't go to dental school to become a content creator.

We've posted a lot of tips on our SmartBox blog for dentists who insist on writing their own dental content. Here's a blog post from January 2017.

Is Your Dental Content Marketing a Help or a Hindrance?

Today's dental landscape is hugely competitive. More and more dentists are using every means at their disposal to get and keep their name in front of their prospects. Content marketing is one very popular way to maintain name recognition and influence new dental prospects.

Dentists are assumed to be competent these days and are therefore considered largely interchangeable. Patients have no reason to choose one dentist over another except for price, insurance, and/or availability.

Content marketing, done well, takes the dentist out of the "herd" and establishes him or her as an expert in the minds of dental prospects. However, Sturgeon's Law, named after science fiction writer Ted Sturgeon, says "90 percent of everything is crap." That rule, unfortunately, applies to online dental content.

How Dental Content Goes Bad

1. **Writing Over Their Heads**
   Far too much content about dental conditions and treatments is written though it was for other dentists. Technical terms and jargon have no place in online dental content unless they're explained in simple terms.

   Content that is written with a complete disregard for the reading level of the audience is an immediate turnoff.

2. **Producing Content That Reeks**
   Stale, dated, poorly researched, and poorly written content does more harm than good. Your patients and prospects deserve the most accurate, up-to-date, engaging, and trustworthy content you can provide. There are no shortcuts to producing good content, but trying to rush the process results in bad content.

3. **Furnishing Non-Original Content**
   One of the ways that dentists try to rush the process of producing content is to buy it. If you've paid a firm for dental content, you should know that what you've been told is content uniquely produced for you almost certainly isn't. That sort of content is sold, and resold, over and over.

   Google is death on identical content that appears on more than one name domain. Only the site on which the content was first indexed gets the SEO credit while the other may actually draw a penalty.

That's the "90 percent" of dental content … crap. Here are four tips to keep your dental content firmly in the top 10 percent.

1. **Keep your audience in mind**
   Writing at a middle school reading level, about 8th grade, is

optimal for the internet. That kind of writing can be difficult. Keep your words small, your sentences short, and use a lot of white space by breaking up paragraphs. There are a number of online readability checkers you can use to determine if your writing will go over your audience's head.

2. **Plan your article or post**

   Relatively few people have a talent for writing well. Good writing takes time, focus, concentration, and a plan. Outline, if that's comfortable for you, and don't be afraid to revise the outline before you begin. In fact, revise the outline as you write if you discover that something's not working for you.

3. **Make your content enjoyable**

   Good writing makes good reading, and good writing includes engaging your audience. Even dental topics can be treated with a light hand without minimizing the importance of what you're writing about. Don't trust your own reaction to your writing; have it read by someone you trust.

4. **State the problem, emphasize the solution**

   Your readers aren't looking for "doom and gloom" in your articles; they're looking for hope. You need to be sure to emphasize that the dental condition you're writing about is treatable. Patient and prospects need to know that they can smile without embarrassment, eat without pain, and enjoy life again. Bad content is everywhere on the internet, but by following these four tips, your dental content can be the exception to Sturgeon's Law.

You've got a challenge ahead of you if you intend to produce your own online content. But if you've got the desire, time, and talent, go for it! You just won't be making any money while you're writing.

You Get Less Than What You Pay For

Many dentists turn to "prepackaged" marketing content to fill the need. There are a couple of overwhelmingly good reasons not to choose this route.

Many marketing firms out there offer packaged dental content. Their pitch is that they'll produce top-quality emails, white papers, ghostwritten books, and so on, **uniquely** for you. And they'll do it all for a ridiculously low price.

Sorry. That just doesn't happen. Writing quality content is a **labor-intensive and time-consuming** prospect, even for professional writers.

Let's say you're looking for a series of emails about dentures to send to the segment that will be most interested in them – seniors. Creating an organized series of 10 to 12 **original** dental emails on a single topic will take most professional writers specializing in dentistry anywhere from a day and a half to two days. If that writer is working for $25 an hour, creating that original series will cost the provider upwards of $700 by the time all the business-related costs are factored in. Add markup, and you could easily spend $1000 to $1,500 for **one** email series to **one segment** of your prospects.

Producing that unique content for just one dentist is prohibitively expensive. These companies get around that by offering the **same** content to a wide number of dentists with suitable rebranding for each practice. Potentially, one cookie-cutter content company can sell that content to **thousands** of dentists. That allows them to reduce the cost to make more sales and a lot more money.

Exactly how many dentists get identical content? Only those marketing firms know for sure. But if you're in a larger market, it's likely that **at least** one other dentist will have **the same packaged content** on his or her website.

That would be embarrassing, yes? But it gets worse.

As you read, Google is absolute death on duplicate content, and that includes largely plagiarized content. Google keeps track of these things, and the **first** dental website to carry that content (regardless of branding) gets the credit and probably a boost in search rankings. All the other websites actually draw a **penalty** in search engine results pages for plagiarism. If it gets bad enough, your website can even be banned from search results!

No matter how good a deal that packaged content seems to be, **you simply can't afford to be lost online**. Steer clear. Do it yourself or outsource it to a reputable firm.

SmartBox has a dedicated team of professional writers to create **fresh and unique** content for our dentists' websites and for their email marketing. We also provide ghostwriting services on the topic(s) of a dentist's choice. And our writers run all of their work through plagiarism checkers to make sure that the content we provide is unique to you.

You've Set Your Hook. Now What?

How often you should send prospects new information?

Too often, and you run the risk of being seen as pushy and annoying. Too seldom, and there's a better-than-even chance that your prospects will choose another dentist.

Scheduling that information to your prospects, who are at different places in your sales funnel, can eat up a lot of a staff person's time. Dental practices that control that information flow manually generally have a raft of spreadsheets to track who is supposed to get what information and when.

There's always that risk that, due to time pressure, miscommunication, or carelessness, your prospects may not receive the information they need. Or they may receive the same information on several occasions. They may even receive information that's not relevant to them.

Even if everything goes well, that additional duty can be a source of stress for one or more of your staff members. Depending on how busy your practice is, maintaining the flow of communication can interfere with other duties, or vice versa.

The solution to staying in front of your patients until they're ready to choose you is to automate your communications.

Automated customer relationship management (CRM) systems are ideal for the purpose.

CRMs provide welcomed and valuable content to prospects and current patients with carefully considered timing. With automation, it's easy to add new releases about developments of interest to them. In addition to condition-specific information, you can weave in general interest information such as dental self-care tips and engaging notes about your practice. Carefully considered timing allows you to remain memorable but not intrusive.

CRMs "drip" information to your prospects until they're ready to decide.

There are a wide variety of CRMs available. They vary in ease of use – some have a pretty steep learning curve – and in the analytics capabilities they offer. Analytics are important because they allow you test which emails, which subject lines, which calls to action, and even which types of clickable links get the best response from your prospects.

Putting together the content of just **one** email with variations in subject lines, calls to action, and clickable links, and then sending that out to a predetermined segment at predetermined times, is quite an undertaking by itself. But can you imagine how much staff time would be required to compile and analyze the results of just one test by hand?

Busy dentists would do well to invest in a CRM. But before you rush out and snag a shiny new system that will take you a couple of months to learn to use, let's take a closer look at what all is involved.

I've been a client of Colin Receveur since 2013.

I already had a prominent web presence.

Colin and his brilliant team were quickly able to consolidate and automate our online programs – email responses, phone tracking and recording, press releases, blog posts, Infusionsoft integration with ortho and implant campaign sequences.

We can measure our results and follow up on leads, as well as add prospects to our funnel.

– Dr. Mitchel Friedman
LINCROFT, NEW JERSEY

Let's Hear from an Expert

Cindy Morus, our Marketing Automation Specialist, appeared with me in the February 2017 episode of the Inside Patient Attraction™ series. Cindy is an Infusionsoft® Certified Consultant. With more than 30 years' experience helping hundreds of businesses realize greater revenue, efficiency, and productivity, she describes herself as "passionate about making life easier for people and helping them achieve more. I love to teach people how to do things better, faster, easier."

Inside Patient Attraction™ February 2017

Welcome to Inside Patient Attraction. I'm Colin Receveur, and on today's episode I want to talk about automation. I hear all these dentists, they're talking about automation, they're talking about, "How do I automate things and make these emails go out? What is this Infusionsoft, Confusionsoft thing?"

Today I'm going to be joined by Cindy Morus, who's one of our automation experts here at SmartBox. I want to show you some real-life implementable examples of what you can do right now to build this automation, how to do it, what to do, and then what the real-life results are from a doctor that put our Patient Attraction System™ to work inside his practice to help him attract more and better patients.

Welcome to the show, Cindy.

Cindy: Hey Colin, thanks for having me.

Colin: Appreciate you being here. You've got a cute little saying that you use when you're talking about automating things. Tell me what that is.

Cindy: I say, "No more boring, tedious, or annoying. Automate it."

Colin: No more sending out one-off emails, and no more spreadsheets, and tracking things? If it can be kept track of, it can be automated in a sense, that you don't have to touch it anymore.

Cindy: That's right, and those are kind of cues to people when they start to feel that. That they can say to me, "Hey, what are we going to do about this? How can we automate it?"

Colin: Cool, cool. Tell me about – you can do simple stuff, you can do complex stuff; tell me about the range of things that you can automate within Infusionsoft.

Cindy: Yeah, so, by the way, Infusionsoft isn't the only tool we use for automation. There's also Active Campaign, another tool that we use. There's a lot of them out there, different costs, different abilities. These are the two that we've chosen to use with our doctors.

Colin: Pretty cool.

Cindy: The most common thing that you'll see is where you have a little box on the website, where somebody will give you their first name and email address. That gets them into your system, and you have permission to send them automated emails. Then you can, what we do is we have a series of emails, educational emails that go out to the patients on a weekly basis, educating them about the doctors services, and getting a comfortable relationship going with the dentist before they might ever come in.

Colin: How often are you sending out these emails once you get them into the system? How often are you contacting patients?

Cindy: Generally on a weekly basis.

Colin: For months, forever?

Cindy: Oh, it depends. The doctor approves how many go out. We have some material that they can look at and make some changes, and approve it. Some of the auto-responder sequences are 10 emails, some of them are close to 20. It depends on how much it takes to tell the story.

Colin: To get the patient to know, like, and trust you.

Cindy: That's right.

Colin: That's really what it comes down to, is know, like, and trust.

Cindy: That's right.

Colin: How do you know that it's working?

Cindy: Well, of course we track everything here for our dentists, and we track how many people come to the website, how many people sign up, how long they stay before they unsubscribe, when they actually call into the office, how many people are opening them and clicking on different things. We can track all of that.

Colin: Very cool. Tell me about – how do you create these automated sequences, Cindy? What goes into putting them together, and making them work for the dentist?

Cindy: Oh, that's a good question. First we start with creating the icon in our program, whether it's Infusionsoft or Active Campaign; that is the box that they fill in. There's code on that, that I give to our web development team, and they put it onto the website, and they make it look all pretty.

Then after that, there's a thank you page that they go to. For most of the auto-responder sequences, we send them to another form where they can fill in if they would like to receive a printed copy of the special report. Then there's a thank you page for that. Then after that, they've entered into the automation, and they start to get the emails.

They'll get the first email, and then we put a timer in to make it wait seven days until the next email goes out. We do that all the way through to the end.

Colin: They just get one a week until the end of time?

Cindy: That's right, and it's totally hands off. We notify the dentist office when someone signs up for, just puts in their email. Then we also send them the special report, and the mailing address if the person wants to get a copy of it.

Colin: Then what about creating all these reports, and emails, and content? Who does that?

Cindy: Oh yeah, that's a big job. Fortunately I don't do that. I just take what they give me. We do have a department that handles all of our writing. Then they give it to me, and then I customize it and make sure that it's exactly what the doctors approved. Then it's totally hands off, there's nothing that needs to be done.

They can sign up ... You know, people are searching day and night. I actually went through this recently myself, and since we do dental marketing, I tested them. I called several, and one sent me an email about a week later and said, "Are you a patient?" I said, "No."

Colin: A week later?

Cindy: Yes.

Colin: Oh, wow.

Cindy: A whole week.

Colin: Well, you were gone by then.

Cindy: Well, I had chosen someone else, obviously.

Colin: Yeah.

Cindy: I called a couple more, sent a couple emails, I just wanted to see, do a little market research out in Sacramento and see what would happen. Someone got back to me very quickly, and turned out actually to be a very close dentist. I really enjoyed going. It worked out to my benefit, but I did kind of monitor what they were doing. It wasn't what we do with dentists, what our dentists do.

Colin: What you found was that the majority of these dentists that you reached out to didn't even try to contact you back within any reasonable urgency or amount of time?

Cindy: No.

Colin: I mean, that's something that I know at least on previous podcasts we've talked about, with returning phone calls. New patients don't leave voicemails, new patients aren't going to send you an email and wait around for a week. You've got to have an automated system in place to handle this.

Cindy: Right.

Colin: So that you're not losing these new patients. I mean, that's just ...

Cindy: Right, and they didn't even bother to look and see if I was a patient, or call me. I left them all the bread crumbs so that they could get in touch with me.

Colin: It's just laziness.

Cindy: Yeah, or lack of systems, lack of automation.

Colin: Sure, sure. What, you know you've done so many of these. Is there one doctor that really stands out in your mind as like a flagship of somebody that we can talk about, that these doctors that are watching the webinar today can go out and check out, or really see hands-on what this is all about?

Cindy: I would have them go look at Dr. Feder's site, he's in Illinois.

Colin: Tom Feder in Illinois.

Cindy: Right, he had 50 to 60 patients a month coming in before he started working with us, and now he's at 70 to even over 100 new patients a month.

Colin: He had a 22 to one ROI with us, 2,200 percent return on investment.

Cindy: Yeah, take that to the bank.

Colin: Take it all the way to the bank.

Cindy: Right, and of course it's all automated. He's not having to go out there and produce the content, he's not having to go out and send out the emails, it's all happening while he's still working, or he's asleep, or he's with his family.

Colin: All part of the Patient Attraction System™.

Cindy: That's right.

Colin: What are these campaigns based on? What are you targeting? Why does somebody want to get these emails from you?

Cindy: Well, if they're searching on the internet, they're looking for information. There's a lot of information out there of course, and they're probably finding some of it. This way, the way that we write it is not only educational, but it's really caring. It shows that we're interested in them, and it helps them to get to know us. We know going to the dentist isn't high on people's list of fun things to do, or their bucket list.

Colin: I don't think it's on the list at all, yeah.

Cindy: Some people are afraid, and have had bad experiences. We try to deal with the things that we know that patients are uncomfortable about, or that they just don't know, and give them really good, caring information.

Colin: These areas that we're trying to educate them on, we're talking about the niches in industry. The patient's looking for something specific. Maybe it's sedation, or maybe it's implants, or maybe it's orthodontics, or maybe it's Invisalign, or whatever it could be.

Cindy: That's right. We're even working on some now with sleep apnea.

Colin: We have that new sleep apnea survey that we've rolled out.

Cindy: That's right, it's a quiz. It asks, I don't know, eight or 10 questions, and the people score themselves one, two, or three. Then it actually calculates their risk factor for sleep apnea. Our goal in that particular sequence is, first of all they get sorted when they come into the automation, so they get different emails. Again, we're segmenting the list, we're targeting and talking to the people. If you're low risk, then we're not going to, we're going to give you different information than if you're high risk.

Our goal for that is to have them come in for a consult so we can work with them on it, because we know how dangerous sleep apnea is.

Colin: Yeah.

Cindy: We're sharing that in the emails. That we know about it, we care about it, and we know that if you have it, you're miserable, your family's miserable, and your health is in danger.

Colin: Yeah. For anybody that's watching this webinar here, for tonight and tonight only, whether you're a current client, a past client, or not even yet a client, I want to make a very special offer to you, that if you want to see what one of these Patient Attraction Systems™ that we've built, like the kind we use for Dr. Feder, and all these different dentists that are killing it right now in their market areas, I want to offer a 50 percent off promo to let you kind of dabble your toe in the water and see what it's all about. Shoot me a personal email, my email address is colin@smartboxwebmarketing.com.

Shoot me an email, I'll send you back the link to the special order form where you can get this 50 percent, $2,000 off order form to get a customized Patient Attraction System™ built for your practice.

Thanks for being here Cindy, I appreciate you being on the show.

Cindy: Thanks, Colin.

Colin: Coming all the way from Sacramento to visit us, and talk about how we can help doctors to attract more and better patients. Appreciate everybody here watching tonight. Keep moving forward.

Some Marketing Dollars Work Harder Than Others

Follow-up gets dental prospects to pick up the phone and book an appointment, which is exactly what your marketing should accomplish. When that happens, there are two important considerations: How did they find your practice, and how many new prospects are being appointed?

To maximize your marketing ROI, you need to know what parts of your marketing are working best. And every new qualified prospect that isn't appointed is a waste of your marketing dollars.

When it comes to discovering what parts of your marketing mix are bringing in the most new patients, and how good a job your phone answerers are doing, phone tracking is the undisputed champion. As you'd suspect, phone tracking is the basis of the Fourth Pillar – Tracking.

Our daily phone log, and recorded calls into our internet phone number, we've been very pleased with.

And our website is beautiful—you've done one heck of a great job.

– Dr. Randy Schmidt
CHICAGO, ILLINOIS

Survival Strategies

1 90-95 percent of prospects who visit your website aren't ready to choose a dentist. You have to stay in front of them until they're ready to "buy."

2 Offer incentives – a white paper, a book, or something else of value – in exchange for their email addresses.

3 Follow up by sending useful information that addresses their problems over time.

4 Creating the content to fill each follow-up "stream" for different segments is a huge undertaking and a waste of your time and talents.

5 Duplicate online content, which is most purchased content, is a major negative as far as Google is concerned. Just don't do it.

6 Timing is crucial when it comes to following up with prospects. Invest in customer relationship management software and automate the process.

9

THE FOURTH PILLAR: TRACKING

New patients have found you, like and trust you, and have chosen you.

Exactly HOW did that happen?

Most dental practices make some effort to find out how their new patients discovered them. Generally, the practice phone answerers will ask, or the receptionist when the patient comes in for the appointment.

Studies show that patients are notoriously unreliable when it comes to identifying what part of your marketing is responsible for them becoming your patients. The data you're getting from your new patients is hopelessly flawed. You may be left with the impression that your newspaper ads are bringing them in when, in fact, your website is delivering the vast majority.

Too many dentists, when asked how they're marketing is doing, will answer, "Well, I feel like it's working okay." I'm a small business owner, like you. One of the things I learned really fast is that "feelings" are no way to run a business.

The end goal of your marketing should be to put more patient butts in chairs and to realize the maximum ROI while you're doing it. Few dentists can afford to throw money away on marketing channels that aren't working. Every dollar of your marketing budget has to work for you.

Without an automated system in place to **accurately** track your marketing's effectiveness, you're wasting tons of money on what doesn't work.

That Phone's Gotta Ring

Website-originated appointment requests are easy to track. But much more often, appointments start with a phone call. Fortunately, you don't have to rely on patient self-report to find out what's working in your marketing.

Tracking the actual source of every incoming phone call is the ideal way to determine the effectiveness of every part of your marketing. You can't rely on your phone answerers to keep track for several reasons. The first is that they're relying on patient self-report, which is inaccurate at best. Second, in many practices the phone answerers are wearing more than one hat – they're also the front office staff or even dental hygienists taking a turn in the barrel.

The only certain way to track the source of your new patient phone calls is to automate the process.

SmartBox provides several automated phone tracking systems for our dentists. Each marketing vehicle in a dentist's marketing program is assigned a different phone number. All those numbers are routed to the practice phones.

The source of each incoming call is automatically tracked and the call itself is recorded. That information is stored in an easily accessible database. Why record the calls? The last crucial step in the patient attraction process is converting new patient callers to scheduled appointments. The skill of the phone answerers determines success or failure. Our dedicated team of Call Quality Analysts reviews incoming calls to see if the office staff's phone protocol is scheduling or losing patients.

Very few if any of the dentists I've spoken with – thousands – believe that their phone answerers are doing anything other than a bang-up job appointing new patients. If only that were true.

SmartBox tracked and analyzed the incoming calls to every one of our Elite level dentists for an entire quarter. What we found was cause for concern.

On average, among our Elite dentists, a whopping **54-77 phone calls a month weren't answered during business hours.** You might not think that's a big deal, but if 20 percent of those calls were new patients with an average case value of $1,500, then those dentists are losing $16,500 to $22,500 a month in new business!

Dental practices were also **failing to appoint** significant numbers of dental prospect callers. That's more money out of their pockets and more wasted marketing dollars.

We couldn't have that, so we decided to do something about it.

Let's Hear from an Expert

Rachel Reeves is SmartBox's Sales Director and an expert in closing the deal. Not only that – she uses her extensive knowledge and skills to help SmartBox dentists convert many more new prospect calls to appointed patients. She joined me in March 2017 for our Inside Patient Attraction™ episode to discuss how dentists' phone answerers can make a practice much more successful with the right training.

Inside Patient Attraction™ March 2017

Colin: As a patient attraction company, it's a rare occurrence when I'm going to tell any of our listeners that I can double or even triple your new patients without spending another dime on marketing, but today I'm going to make a rare exception, and I want to show you how to put more butts in your chairs, double or even triple your current new patient flow without spending another dime on marketing or advertising or websites or SEO.

It's great to have you on board, Rachel.

Rachel: I'm happy to be here, Colin. Thanks for having me on.

Colin: We're going to talk a little bit today about phone training and what it means to these doctors, because it's not really just phone training, you know. We see so many doctors that spend all these thousands and thousands and hundreds of thousands of dollars on marketing, and they never get a return from it. Today, I want to talk about why that is and how having a great front desk can fix that, can play that role of actually making your marketing get more results.

Rachel: When we're looking at marketing and how it works, we look at key performing indicators, and for us at SmartBox, number one is calls. Right? When you're looking at how many calls come in, the next thing that you look at is how that person answers the phone and are they able to appoint that prospective patient.

Colin: In all the doctors that I've talked to over all the years, I've never once had a doctor that said to me, "Colin, my front desk sucks. They don't appoint any patients. They need training." I've never once had a doctor actually admit that their front desk was bad. Have you ever had that happen to you?

Rachel: Not really, per se, them saying that, but I have had them say, you know, "Jessica may need some help," or "It sounds like Sarah, basically, she just doesn't like the world today," or something in that nature, but not specifically their entire staff.

Colin: I feel like what happens a lot of times is a lot of doctors, they go through, they do a training course. There's a lot of big-ego phone trainers out there that do a lot of rah-rah, and they go through this course, and they get this certificate on the wall, and then *poof*, they're trained, they're done, and they never follow up on it. There's nobody holding that front desk accountable ongoing to make sure that they're still producing the results. What we've designed our program to do is to be an ongoing, certify and keep your staff up-to-date with as many people, your entire front staff certified for life, online curriculum that you can access any time, and we back it up with monitoring your phones, listening to them, and making sure that your staff is held accountable, because if you don't hold people accountable, it doesn't do a whole lot.

Rachel: Right. Yeah. I totally agree. I mean, to me it's all about, you can start a conversation with somebody and guide them through to the result and make sure that when they hang up, they feel good about it. That's what SmartBox does. We start with how are they answering the phone. Do they sound like they just woke up, or do they sound mad because they're hungry? Are you feeding your employees? Are they getting to take a lunch? You know.

Colin: You hit an interesting thing there. One of the big hurdles that we see a lot is the front desk taking lunches, because your highest call volume for new patients is going to occur around the lunchtime, from 10:30 to 2:30, and when you have front desks that are out for lunch, you have calls not getting answered. New patients aren't going to leave a message.

Rachel: No.

Colin: They're not going to call you back. They're not going to leave a voicemail for you to check. They're not going to wait around and hope it works out. They're going to go right down that list to the next provider or the next dentist and make a phone call, and you lost them. Some of the most effective practices that I've seen, in terms of appointing patients and training their staff, have a ruthless staff meeting once a week, and they actually pull the recorded calls off the answering machine, and they pick two or three or four recorded calls, and they play them and constructively critique them as a group in the staff meeting on a weekly basis. It's ruthless, but it's constructive, and it's positive, and it's making positive changes, not saying "Oh, Sally. You suck," but "Sally, hey. You did this, but it would have been better if you'd handled it X, Y, Z."

Rachel: Absolutely. Yeah. I think that's crucial, and I think that kind of goes back to the culture of a practice. I think that it's important that you slow down and you realize that one call could be worth, we set an average patient at around $1,500 here at SmartBox, so if somebody doesn't give us that in the information …

Colin: That's for a general dentist.

Rachel: That's a general dentist. Now, I would say upward in the way of $4,500 to 6,000 for specialties, but what happens is that when you're talking to that person on the phone, they're not just a prospect for that one specific service. They could bring in their aunt or their cousin or whoever.

Colin: Absolutely. Excellent.

Rachel: I think of us. My mom has 10 brothers and sisters. If I brought in all of them, you know, that's a huge return.

Colin: That's why we're … I mean, part of our phone training, we're big bat-line proponents. If you don't know the bat-line principle, give us a call and talk to us.

We'll give you a little tidbit without selling you the whole program, but the bat-line concept is critical for new patient scheduling, because you can't be juggling four balls in the air, and then you take that new patient phone call and expect to give them your undivided attention and focus on them and lead to a positive result.

Rachel: That's absolutely the truth, and so it's really, to me, it's important to be able to not only control the call but control your own emotions and your own environment, what's going on around you. Things may get busy. You need to be able to stop and give undivided attention to that bat line, per se, because that is a prospective patient that could be bringing in, you know, upward of hundreds of thousands of dollars for the practice.

Now, we don't look at them as dollars. We look at them as people, but it's important, it's really important to realize that if you don't answer that call and to the best of your ability, somebody else will, and they'll persuade them.

Colin: Somebody else will. They will. They will. That's one thing that ... You know, you look at corporate dentistry. You look at the large dental practices that have grown, privately owned, right? Both of them have something in common. They have great systems. They have great training in place. It's not all about the marketing resources and their big gorilla-in-the-room tactic. It's that they do have good training and they do have good systems. Both of those come down to the phones. How are you going to handle and appoint, what's the management structure inside your office, and making sure that you are appointing as close to that optimal number. You know, we shoot for about 80 percent. We want 90 percent of calls to be answered, and we want to appoint 80 percent of the new patients that call. That's our bar.

Rachel: Yeah.

Colin: If you want that to happen, it comes down to systems and management and training.

Rachel: Yeah. I could not agree more.

Colin: And accountability.

Rachel: And accountability. One thing that I actually really love about our brand is that it is a system, so you're working with all of the different components, tactics, capabilities, per se, that will move your business forward.

Colin: Mm-hmm.

Rachel: To me, it's real important ... I think one of the reasons we're adding this as a capability, per se, to our suite of products is that it's just as important as the beginning part of a consumer's path. It's just as important as the engagement side of things. This is basically where you take them and you nurture them and you move them on.

Colin: Absolutely.

Rachel: If this doesn't happen, then you're going to miss out. It's a key factor in the consumer's path.

Colin: I think one thing that's been a little backwards in the dental industry so far is there are some other industry experts out there that say you should do the phone training first, and that's going to get you new patients, but phone training doesn't make your phone ring. Right?

Rachel: Correct.

Colin: I think that's something that is a little bit of a misperception in the world, marketing first, and then you move the golf ball down the garden hose, per se. Right?

Rachel: Mm-hmm.

Colin: As the consumer's path, if you want to call it that, as they're coming toward you advertising, marketing, then phone training, and then interoffice systems, and then you look at your backend office systems. Right?

Rachel: Yeah.

Colin: That's the consumer's path for how you need to be training your office, because you got to get the patients in the door. If you get so caught up on the back end and then the front end, your new patient supply dries up and all of a sudden, you have a cash problem, and you don't want that to happen. Always work consumer path down is what I practice and preach to our dentists.

Rachel: Yeah. I could not agree more.

Colin: One of the most important parts of the entire phone call that happens between the doctor's office and the patient is the close, right, that point that you actually appoint them. Part of our teaching is based on Robert Cialdini, who many of you watching this are probably familiar with. If you've followed me for any length of time, you know I'm a huge Cialdini fan. It's all about psychology, right, what we call the dual alternative close, saying, "Would you like to come in for an appointment on Tuesday or Wednesday?" You're giving that prospect the choice, but you're really not giving them a choice. "You're coming in to see me either way" is the psychology component of that, and that's critical. You know you have the greeting and all these different parts that we train and hold your staff accountable for, but then the close is one of the most important parts. Tell me a little bit about that, Rachel.

Rachel: The close is extremely important. You're engaging and you're building rapport throughout the entire conversation with the prospective patient, and it's so important that when you get to that point, you know you have them. You have them kind of hooked, and they like you, and they're interacting with you a little bit. At that point, you say "Great. I'm looking forward to meeting you. Could you come in today, or could you come in tomorrow? I can get you in at 2 o'clock tomorrow. Does that work?" Basically, you're answering questions that they might ask and overcoming questions that could be thrown at you, making them feel more secure as they move forward, because they don't even have to ask. You've already answered it for them.

Colin: What kind of results have you seen working with some of our clients with their phone training specifically?

Rachel: I've seen great results with a lot of doctors. One of the ones most recently is out of Texas, and they were kind of … The girls were just not as confident in their approach. Started working with them on, basically, how to kind of lift their tone a little bit and to sound a little bit more abrasive when they're talking and to control the conversation. That helped them tremendously. They went from like setting about 40 percent of the calls that were coming in to setting almost 75 percent of the calls within about a two-and-a-half month period.

Colin: Wow.

Rachel: What that means is that relationships do matter. The way you talk to somebody does matter.

Colin: How you make them feel.

Rachel: How you make them feel. If I answer the phone, and I say, "SmartBox Dental Practice," you know, "This is Rachel," or if I say "SmartBox Dental Practice. This is Rachel. How can I help you?" There's quite a bit of a difference there in how I just greeted that person. It's just really important to be conscientious of the way you sound and, too, of what you say as you move forward in the conversation and listen for just a second to try to understand what is it that they really need.

Are they needing it now because they're in pain? Are they needing it now because they chipped their front tooth and they're embarrassed? You know, and you shoot right at that.

Colin: Back to the results. You said they were at 40 percent, and now they're at 70 percent?

Rachel: Them? Yeah, about 75 percent.

Colin: An 80 percent increase …

Rachel: Yes.

Colin: … in new patients without another dime spent on marketing. That's just in appointing the calls that are already occurring at a higher percentage.

Rachel: Absolutely. Yes.

Colin: Well, that's phenomenal.

Rachel: It is phenomenal, and that makes my day when that happens, because it means we're doing our job. You know, we don't need to continue to ask for more and more investment to get to move the needle up. You know, we get to help you with that.

Colin: I know I was looking at a doctor out of New York that, again, like I said earlier, thinks his call team is so awesome, thinks there's no problems with them. He thinks that they've been trained and they're great, and during business hours, he's answering 40 percent of his phone calls coming in. During business hours.

Rachel: Wow.

Colin: Unbelievable. It's not always the percentage you're appointing, but I've seen so many doctors that their staff, whether they're understaffed or it's during lunchtime, whatever it may be, they're just flat out not answering calls.

Rachel: Yeah. Well, I'd have to give them another one of my sayings, which is, "I love you more than your feelings, doctor, and we need to look at this." That's unacceptable.

Colin: Absolutely. Absolutely. You know, one thing that we offer as part of our phone training that I don't know anybody else in the industry does is we back it up with a guarantee.

Rachel: Yeah.

Colin: The guarantee that we offer with our phone training is if you come into our program, if we accept you into our program, and you're already answering 90 percent of your phone calls, and you're already appointing them at 80 percent, once we do our baseline, we'll give you your money back, and I'll personally send you a check for 500 bucks. That's us putting our money where our mouth is, if so many dentists that think they're doing so well, and they don't even realize the opportunity that they're missing.

Rachel: Yeah.

Colin: They don't see it. It's in their blind spot.

Rachel: Yeah. There's always room for improvement. I think with any skill, there's always room for improvement.

Colin: Absolutely.

Rachel: It's that ability to be humble and willing that will make a huge difference for practices across the United States, is to try something different, and to hold each other accountable. I like that you've said that a few times, because if peers hold each other accountable, just think how much further the practice is going to go. I mean …

Colin: Oh, absolutely. We're opening up our next training curriculum with the phone training program here in about 45 days, so if anybody has interest in getting on, feel free to give us a call, shoot us an email. Be glad to give you more information about signing up during our next open enrollment period.

Rachel: Yeah. I would love to work with some new doctors or existing doctors.

Colin: Awesome. Yeah, or existing. Well, it's been great to have you on the show, Rachel.

Rachel: Thanks, Colin.

Colin: Thanks for coming and hanging out a little bit, and as always, keep moving forward.

Phone tracking, the Fourth Pillar of the Patient Attraction System™, allows dentists to get objective data on what's working and to adjust the marketing budget accordingly.

Dentists can maximize the number of new patients and their marketing ROI.

The Least Expensive Patient You Can Get

Once you have a new patient in your chair, you want to keep them as a long-term patient. That used to be easier.

The barrage of dental marketing doesn't stop just because a new patient made and kept an appointment with your practice. You have to give your new patients good reasons to keep coming back.

Today's dental patients have higher expectations of almost every service provider. They're more attuned to convenience and comfort than any generation that's come before.

The least expensive patient you can get is the one you **already have.**

With that in mind, here's a SmartBox blog post from December 2016 that gives some tips for providing a superior patient experience.

Enhance Your Dental Patients' Experience to Win

What are your dental prospects looking for?

The bottom line is that all of them are looking for someone to solve their dental problems. But there are two distinct groups within your prospects – those who are primarily price- and insurance-driven, and those who aren't.

That second group has the patients **you need to grow your practice and succeed.**

There are many people in the U.S. population with the discretionary income to choose a dentist based on their expectations of a superior outcome, which includes a **superior patient experience.**

That's a crucial distinction in these days of declining insurance reimbursements and increased competition from corporate dentistry. Corporate dentistry is, at its heart, impersonal. It's common for patients who return to the same corporate practice to be seen by different dentists and hygienists. For the price-driven, this isn't a big deal; they assume that dentists are competent and that one is as good as another.

The segment of the population that values a superior experience is looking for a dentist and dental practice that they **trust and relate**

to. When you establish yourself as **the trusted dental expert** who can solve their problems, and your practice as the **preferred choice** for a superior patient experience, those "better" patients will respond.

What Makes a Superior Experience?

People with a large amount of discretionary income seldom stay at budget hotels. They're interested in a certain amount of comfort, agreeable surroundings, and superior amenities and service.

Those people are looking for the same things in your practice. Service begins with their initial contact with your marketing. If they leave a comment on your website or social media, they expect a reply. Otherwise, they expect and appreciate responsive, concerned yet professional service while booking the initial appointment.

Your next opportunity to meet their expectations is when they drive up to your practice. Having a hyper-modern building usually isn't necessary, but your setting should appear reasonably modern and meticulously maintained. The same holds for your reception area/waiting room. Comfortable furniture is a must. Amenities such as a complimentary beverage bar, agreeable music, carefully-tended potted plants, and guest Wi-Fi access count.

Your operatories must be spotless and offer something to distract nervous patients. Windows with nature views are good, as are headphones to allow them to listen to music or in-room television. From a comfort standpoint, warm blankets for the easily chilled and refreshing face towels should be offered.

Above all, the attitude of you and your staff will determine your patient's experience. Expertise is expected; what your better patients want is the sense that they'll **be cared for and taken care of no matter what**. Taking all the time necessary to answer patients' questions and to detail – to the extent that they want – how you'll meet their dental needs and take care of them will help meet those expectations.

Your better patients, the ones who aren't primarily price-driven, are the key to growing your practice, increasing your receipts, and driving your success. Provide these patients with superior experiences, and you'll thrive in spite of the challenge of corporate dentistry.

The Four Pillars of the Patient Attraction System™ create a proven system to attract more and **better** patients over time. And if you're going to stand any chance of holding off the Four Horsemen of Dentistry, you need more and better dental patients. And you need to keep those patients.

I think that the greatest service that SmartBox has added recently is having SmartBox's team listen to and grade our phone calls.

That really eliminates a lot of time for me. I don't have time to go back and listen to all the phone calls.

Ninety percent of them are "change my appointment" or do something simple and just not a valuable use of time.

If I have your team kind of highlighting these calls, "Here's the ones you've got to listen to …" We can grow from that. We can get better answering or fielding those calls, and I can do nothing but help drive new patients in the future.

– Dr. Matthew Burton
CLEARWATER, FLORIDA

Survival Strategies

1. You can't rely on patient self-report to determine what parts of your marketing are bringing in the most new patients.

2. If you don't objectively track your marketing ROI in each channel, you're wasting marketing dollars. You can't afford that; there's a war on.

3. Phone tracking is the ideal solution to the question of actual ROI.

4. Don't assume your phone answerers walk on water. Our data indicate that they're probably costing you big bucks in unappointed new patients.

5. Don't even try to listen to each recorded new patient phone call yourself. You don't have enough time.

6. Dental practice–specific phone training and certification from SmartBox will pay for itself quickly by returning many more new patients.

Afterword
You Can Triumph in the Coming War

No one ever said business was easy. There are too many ifs and not enough certainties. There is one certainty, though: Economies go in cycles, with booms replacing busts and vice versa. It's predicting the timing of the changes that is nearly impossible.

I don't claim to have a crystal ball that foretells the future. What I can do, and what I've laid out in this book, is tell you that there are three very real threats and one potential, likely threat to the survival of your dental practice.

The Four Horsemen of Dentistry are coming. It's only a matter of time before they reach your market. Or perhaps they're already there. I can't pretend to know the dynamics of your particular market.

Frankly, it doesn't matter a great deal. If you're serious about your success and you're ready to do something different to get better, lasting results, the Patient Attraction System™ is the answer to the challenges you face.

Proven, Guaranteed Results from Your Marketing

SmartBox works with more than 550 dentists on three continents to help them get more patients, more profits, and more freedom.

Many SmartBox dentists are realizing enormous returns on their marketing investments – **from 1,700 percent to over 4,600 percent**. Because they're not trying to compete head-to-head against corporate dentistry, because they're attracting not only **more** patients but **better** patients, and because they're viewed as relatable, trustworthy dental experts, they're well positioned to withstand the coming storm.

Are you?

If you're going to war, and all indications suggest you will be, it's better to do it from a position of strength. And the sooner you assume that position, the greater your likelihood of victory.

That position of strength is the **Patient Attraction System™**.

I know that to be true, not only because of the results we get for our dentists but also because SmartBox has had to establish itself against a large number of very well-established marketing firms. We use the same principles of attraction in our own marketing. We're a patient attraction services company, not a dental marketing company. We stand out from the pack, **and it works**.

SmartBox has experienced over 1600 percent growth in three years. My company is a testament to the power of the PAS. It's your secret weapon against the Four Horsemen of Dentistry.

Guaranteed Dental Marketing!

Not only do we get outstanding results for our dentists, but we back our performance with our **$10K Guarantee™**.

Basically, it comes down to this: Depending on the level of service you choose, we guarantee to get you a certain number of new patient phone calls. After the first 12 months of your contract, you can ask for a SmartBox Performance Audit. If we haven't delivered an average number of new patient calls in a consecutive three-month period that meets or exceeds your guarantee, we'll cancel the rest of your contract and send you a check for $10,000.

Here's all you have to do to keep your guarantee in force: 1) get us all the information we need to launch your website within 90 days of signing with us, 2) agree to implement all our marketing suggestion, and 3) answer 90 percent of your phone calls during business hours.

That's it. There are no hidden clauses or "gotchas."

Succeed on Your Own Terms

Every dentist is different, and success for one may be something another dentist would avoid.

Some dentists love to work. Others work with an eye toward retirement, even if that's 30 years or more away. Some dentists structure their schedules to allow for long weekends and ample vacation time during the year. Others resent even one day away from work.

All of those dentists have a different definition of success, and none of them is wrong. Success is a **personal** thing.

By the same token, not all dentists fail in the same way. According to the banks, dental practices have a 0.5 percent failure rate. Those are the practices that go into foreclosure.

There are many other ways to fail as a dentist.

What about the dentist who owns his own practice but works in another practice to afford his lifestyle?

What about the dentist who has to do her own hygiene to survive?

Or the dentist who didn't make any money last year?

What about the dentist who doesn't have enough new patients for him and his associate?

What about the dentist who can't afford to take time off?

We need to rethink our definitions of success AND failure.

We all work so we can play. If we didn't have to work, we'd play all the time. Even the so-called workaholics would probably take a more relaxed approach to work in that case.

What do **you** want out of life? Once you've decided that, **how will you get there?**

There's no right or wrong answer; there's only your answer. But the Patient Attraction System™ has the power to help you succeed on your own terms in spite of the Four Horsemen of the Dental Apocalypse.

> **Again: What do you want out of life?**

One Dentist's Answer

Sometimes, when the stress of owning a small but rapidly growing business gets to me, I listen to this audio podcast. It reminds me of the most important reasons that I do what I do. For me, money is a means to that end. It's not the end-all of my efforts.

"Finding the Best Work-Life Balance"
with Colin Receveur and Dr. David Maloley

Hi, SmartBox founder and CEO Colin Receveur here, and I recently recorded a special audio-only podcast with Dr. David Maloley from Avon, Colorado, in the Vail Valley.

Dr. Maloley, who runs a podcast of his own called "The Relentless Dentist," is a SmartBox client who has a remarkable life story and outlook on life.

Dr. Maloley spent the first half of his life in a small Nebraska town, where he grew up in a house where he could see homes of other family members from his own home. He went to a two-room schoolhouse. It was a very traditional upraising that included seeing adults work six and seven days per week.

Going to dental school, time in the military, and living in Europe changed his perspective on work-life balance. It helped him overcome his workaholic tendencies.

Now he lives where other people vacation, working four days a week and skiing whenever possible with his preschool-aged son. He does it in a market saturated with dentists by staying current in his dentistry and his marketing.

His wife's near-death experience was a "slap in the face" to savor the moment and to live in the present. Now, he wants to share that message with other dentists.

Do you want to be a grandparent who tells the grandkids not to make the mistakes you made, or do you want to tell the stories about the awesome things you did?

What would you do with **more patients, more profits, and more freedom?** Would you spend more time with your family? More time exploring the world? Would you be able to live in the moment?

Hey, this is Colin Receveur here for a special edition of the Patient Attraction Podcast™, and I've got a very special guest on the line who's also been a client of ours for a couple years now, Dr. David Maloley out of Vail Valley, Colorado. Hey, you on the line with me, Dr. Dave?

David: Absolutely, thanks for inviting me.

Colin: Yeah, well you've got an awesome story, Dr. Dave. I know you also have a podcast of your own that you run for dentists. Tell me a little about what you're doing in the podcast world.

David: Well, you know, I think I was an early adopter to podcasting,

I've been on that path of perpetual learning, trying to pick up little gems here and there so that I don't have to learn from the school of hard knocks, so that's gone through cassettes in my car back in undergrad and dental school, through the digital realm. Getting into podcasting, it's all a more entrepreneurial podcast, and the podcast that I really wanted wasn't available, so I've heard lots of entrepreneurs say it, and when people ask me why I started a podcast, the real honest podcast, it goes back to the dramatically incorrect.

I couldn't not do it. Just to provide tips, and tricks, and shared knowledge, I think is the beauty of technology when you think about everyone in the planet being able to enter a conversation. I wanted to be a part of that, and so it certainly pushes my comfort zone as a typical introverted dentist, that broadcasting their voice is a little bit awkward to begin with, but to be able to network with a great minds in dentistry, and people that I've admired for a long period of time, and picked their brains, and the conversation that really is the same conversation I would have if I was having a beer with them. To be able to record that and share that with the world has really been a fun project that I've gone through in the last year and a half or so.

Colin: Today I want to talk with you – when I was out there, for everybody listening, I got to hang out with Dr. Dave for a couple days on a video shoot that we did for his dental practice. Some of the stuff that you shared with me out there off camera about your life story, your work-life balance, and how you came to do what I'll call "celebrate" your life, enjoy your life a lot more than a lot of the dentists that I talked to that are working five, six, seven days a week. Put you on my very short lists of one to do this podcast with today. I really appreciate you being here.

David: I love it, thank you.

Colin: You started out in Nebraska, and I know that your growing-up experience is one contrasting experience that kind of led to your decisions to be where you're at today. Tell me about your life story just to give everybody here some background, and I've got a bunch of questions here as we go through it. I might jump in and cut you off. Tell me your story – how you got to be where you're at now, and what you're doing.

David: Well, I think if you look at the first half of my life, it's certainly planted seeds for a workaholic tendency. I grew up in a small town in Nebraska. Really, most of the houses I could see from my rural house were family. My dad had eleven siblings, all of which – I shouldn't say all of which – most of which lived within maybe five miles of where I live, so cornfields between families is pretty much the existence that I had, and I thought that was normal. My cousins were my friends, they were the people that I looked up to, the people that I hung out with, and amongst that were females who worked really hard to provide for their families. Within the household, very traditional environment. Probably even a little bit retro, I would say, this was in the seventies.

The men, my cousins who were old enough to work, all worked pretty much all day long. That taught me work ethic, it taught me a lot about family support. My grandmother would cook for dozens of people on Sunday and the holiday gatherings were just unbelievable. So I look back at that, and it seems like a dream because it's so different than anyone that I would ever, I don't know anyone living that story today.

So it's really kind of communal living, you know. You didn't ever have a babysitter, you just stayed over with your aunt when your parents needed extra help. That was my initial environment; I grew up going to a two-room schoolhouse. The same one that my father, and all my uncles, and cousins, and aunts went to. It was a real basic lifestyle, it was very simple. My parents weren't afraid to tell me the "Word." I had everything that I ever needed there. I thought that was the way life was; I saw my dad, most his life, work six to seven days a week. A vacation for us was three days off, and now that's what I call every week.

It's pretty amazing when I look back on it; that's where the seeds of work ethic began from, but then through dental school and a military experience, and living in Europe, my system was kind of shocked the other way, and I think between the two ends of the spectrum, I did an okay job overcoming some of that workaholic tendencies, and now living in the Vail Valley, I can see Beaver Creek from my house, essentially. To be able to ski every weekend – and that ended up being the vision for when we started up the practices. Why not do it now, and why not live where other people vacation, and make your life kind of an ongoing vacation?

Colin: Awesome, awesome. So you did a little overseas time as well, I know you were saying. My experience, I was over in Italy, and I think we joke that … I remember guys, they'd open up at about nine in the morning and take lunch at eleven, and have a little fiesta, and come back to work at three to four, or five, and that was it for the day. What was your experience overseas with their lifestyle versus what you saw in Nebraska?

David: Well, all you really see will know that that workaholic tendency proves low when you're in dental school, so that didn't stop. I went to dental school on a health professions scholarship. So I did another residency, which again is kind of 24/7 at least in mind, and then after that I got an assignment to Germany, and to be honest, growing up in Nebraska, when I got orders to go to Germany, I really felt like they were sending me to another planet. I was intimidated, I didn't know, as far as my wife, having employment over there, how that would work. This pushed my comfort zone way too far, and I actually asked for another assignment. If anyone is familiar with the Army, orders are orders; it's not a suggestion. I ended up in a military … it was a med company, which is essentially a deployable dental unit in Germany, right when we were going after it in Afghanistan and Iraq.

So that was always looming. I didn't actually ever deploy. There are some reassignments, later on that I'll tell you a little about when we got to move to Italy. The second I got to Germany, I'd just feel like life was completely different than I was used to there, not just with the cultural things, food, but it was just the way people lived their life.

I remember this little restaurant that we used to frequent, talk about mom-and-pop. It was mom, brother, sister, husband, and maybe an occasional employee that ran this fantastic little restaurant. But the thing that struck me was it was always packed, and they were always turning customers away. There was no, like, "There will be a 20-minute wait." Either you were seated, or you weren't.

The most amazing thing was all of August, they would close down, and they would go to the beach. I thought initially, "This is insane, this is stupid. Like, why won't they expand their facility, why won't they expand their hours? Why would they take a month off? There's so much opportunity."

And it took me a while to really understand the genius – they live below their means, only the ultra-wealthy in America would ever take a month at the beach, right? But this was their lifestyle ongoing, so the work-play balance, that was my first real memory of that.

And then I remember also being over there and flipping through the channels, and I ended up being caught on an interview with George Clooney, and they asked him a question that wasn't an amazing question, and I don't even know that it was an amazing answer, but it just slapped me upside the head. They asked him why he lived in Italy, why he spends so much time in Italy, what does he appreciate over what would be a Hollywood lifestyle, and he said he was filming – I don't remember what movie it was, not that it really matters – but he was filming there, and I'm sure he had a nice luxury condo on the lake there, in Lake Como, and he remembers opening up the shutters, and he looked out on the street and it was the evening time. As he told the story, there were three people, all of worker class, construction worker types, and they were all walking home from work, and every single male had a bottle of wine, a loaf of fresh bread, and a bouquet of flowers. He told about how shocking that experience was, because these weren't wealthy people, it wasn't anyone's birthday, or anniversary, it wasn't a holiday, it was a Tuesday. He said, "I realized that these Europeans know how to celebrate life."

It made me realize how kind of ridiculous the delayed life plan is, and waiting to retirement when you may have more money but you have less energy, and how traditionally we'll postpone life beyond the years when the prime of our lives, really we'll spend working.

I later moved to Italy and really experienced that firsthand because it's very much a culture of a domani – worry about it tomorrow, what are you so stressed about? I remember neighbors there saying, "Come for coffee," in the middle of the day, and of course as an American, you'd say, "No, no I can't. I've got a to-do list." They just would shake their heads, and they would say, "Due minuti, two minutes. Just come in and have a cup of coffee, what's wrong with you?" A lot of that played into when I finally got into private practice and realizing that even though I wanted to live in America long-term, that I needed to find a place that had more of a European lifestyle, and that's ultimately what led us to taking the big risk and starting a practice here in the mountains of Colorado.

Colin: How did you pick Vail Valley? Kind of in the middle of nowhere. How did you go from Italy to the middle of Colorado up in a ski resort town? How did you arrive at that location?

David: Well, there's a chapter to the story that I think is important. Keep in mind, we were living in Italy, there's no dinner and a movie in Italy. You just sit at dinner all night long, so multiple courses, fantastic wine … Sitting at dinner from eight to 11 kind of became a norm for the weekends. While we were overseas, my wife got her doctorate online, and she was recruited to join a startup with a tech startup in Charlotte, North Carolina. I'd always promised her since she followed my career for the first handful of years, that the next phase was hers, and that I would find a dental opportunity wherever she wanted to go.

We left Italy to join – let's just call it the American dream, or what we thought was the American dream. I remember one Friday, startup pace means you're building equity, but there's not really a solid paycheck or predictable paycheck coming in. It's kind of delayed gratification at its height, and I remember one Friday, sitting at home at 10:30 at night, and calling Karen up and saying, "It's time to go home, this is ridiculous." We were fully invested in that lifestyle, we had bought a house right off the bat, beautiful two-porch home, you could walk to the movies from where we were. Really started buying into the tangible things, and we soon started regretting that we weren't into that.

Going back to European lifestyle, they savor experiences as opposed to the tangible things that are parked in the garage, and sit in your living room, all that sort of things. If there's such thing as fail fast, we did it there, we quickly realized that it seemed like life was slapping us upside the head and said, "Why did you jump into this?" I had an awesome opportunity that I was working as an associate there, but I quickly knew that it was time for me to launch off on my own. We looked at probably 12 or 15 different practices in North Carolina, started looking in the city – no, that wasn't for us. We started looking in the mountains in North Carolina. I grew up in Nebraska, my wife in Kansas, and we said, "If we're going to live in the mountains, let's just go for it."

We started looking at Colorado, but again, all the opportunities were in Collins, Colorado Springs, Denver. As we were looking, we had a few days off, and we decided to spend the Fourth of July weekend, 2009, in the mountains, and had a nice hotel in Vail. Just happened across a dusty little space that was obvious to me that is was being marketed as a commercial space, but you could tell by the setup that it was once a dental space. It seemed like, it's something that I looked into, but it didn't seem like the opportunity. We saw that, we were here for Fourth of July, and Vail, it was magical, kind of old-school traditional parade with floats, and fireworks. It felt like I was back in Europe, and I'd never been here.

Literally within 24 hours, maybe 48 hours if I'm stretching it, Karen and I just really started to entertain the thought of starting a practice here. It wasn't good economic times, there were plenty of dentists. They weren't begging for dentists up here, currently saturated market. The thing that drove the point home was that must've been the fifth or sixth of July, we looked at the most perfect dental opportunity you can find, a practice that had low competition, was associate-driven. To take it to the next level, it just needed an owner within it that really put their heart and soul into it.

On paper it looked like the ideal opportunity, and Karen I looked at ourselves and said, "If we buy that practice, near Fort Collins, it's only the 15-year plan to get back into the Vail area." It made no sense on paper, I can tell you getting the loans, securing the property, getting the banks to buy in. I thought, "I'm a dentist. They'll give me whatever I want." Well, when you're upside down in a house in North Carolina, and walking into a saturated market with a sputtering economy, you have to fight some currents certainly, but we were committed to it.

Between July and December that year, we made it happen, and opened our practice in 2009. It wasn't an easy road, to be honest. I learned a lot about marketing, and I learned a lot about myself. My wife just happened to get pregnant as we were starting up, so it went from one mouth to feed, or two mouths to feed, to three mouths to feed pretty quick. That ended up being a blessing in disguise, and I think part of life's design, its purpose in having an infant son looking up at you, and wondering how you're going to provide for them – I'm pretty passionate, and I'm a pretty hard driver, but that really pours fuel in the fire to make sure that you set things up right and that you don't have to worry in the long-term about the search of things.

Colin: They grow up too fast, you said yours is in preschool now, or kindergarten, I'm sorry.

David: Yeah, he's in preschool now, but we're going through the kindergarten research and just figured out where he's going to be going to school. Starting the practice five years ago, and seeing him born five years ago, it's a blink of the eye that days and weeks just seem to go by faster and faster.

Colin: Yep. No kidding, no kidding. Tell me about your balance now, what are you doing in the practice, or what are you doing to enjoy life? Other than the obvious, I see pictures of you and your boy on Facebook all the time skiing and enjoying the slopes out there. I got to say, I'm a little jealous of that. Tell me about your balance now, and what you enjoy doing.

David: In full disclosure, I still have to fight off the seeds of being a

Afterword

workaholic. I love doing the podcasts, I love working in the practice. Work is part of who I am. Rest, and recovery, and enjoying your family, and pausing, I think is what the mountains are really good for. Vail has become a year-round resort, my practice is actually in Avon. At the beginning I did whatever it took, I didn't have full schedules right off the bat, I learned marketing as a necessity, I learned how to make the phone ring.

Once I knew that we were at the point where I could relax a little bit, I went from really seven days a week, not that I ran a full schedule on Saturday and Sunday, but if the phone rang with an emergency, I was there. Now I try and keep my workload to Monday through Thursday, and have three-day weekends, some four-day weekends. I can bike, I can hike right out my back door. Beaver Creek is within a few minutes of where I live, Vail is within 10 minutes of where I live. When I'm on the chair with people who've spent all year trying to get five days in Vail, I really appreciate what I have here in my back door. This has been the best ski season ever, there's only a couple weeks left, but I have close to 30 days on the mountain. Most of that has been with my son, who went from seemingly forgetting every single thing he's learned in ski school last year, to skiing some pretty complicated black ruins all in one year. To see that growth curve and be able to spend some time with him, teaching, but also having that father-son relationship, has been spectacular.

Not to mention part of the story that really drives this home is about a year and a half ago, I was seeing patients just like any other day. Thankfully, this would be the only time I'd ever say this, but thankfully my patient wasn't profoundly numb, so I boosted up the anesthetic, and went back to my private office where my wife was working. She doesn't work there every day, but she was working there that day. She was facedown on her computer, and I thought she was just a little tired. When she looked up at me with this blank stare and couldn't communicate, I knew within a minute or so that she was ... I didn't know that she had a stroke, but I know that she was having stroke-like symptoms.

A long journey from that, she did have a stroke. They performed a lifesaving procedure, and put stents in her neck, and her carotid artery to save her life. For a couple days there, I had to look at, what would life be as a single parent, what would I do with the practice without her support, am I going to be able to bring her home, if she does survive, what will it be like? If there's a message that I can drive home, I think the story that I can share is that my life has been a lot of slaps in the face about you're not living right, but this is the ultimate one.

Life will take you on tangents, but if you don't design it and savor the moment, you just never know when life is going to throw you that ultimate curveball. It's easy to live in the past, it's easy to live in the future, but we really all just need to live in the present. When the most important person in your life is in a life-or-death situation, you realize that work is important, the practice is important, your patients are important. Even myself today, spend way too much time worrying about that and not really being fully present with the people that you love. That ultimate shock has made the last year and a half, time that I really spend a lot of time in contemplation and making sure that I'm living right, and that I'm treating the people in my world right, and that we're taking time to really enjoy the things and the experiences, and most importantly, the people around us because you'll never know when that's taken away.

To me, the saddest story that I ever hear is that older dentist that is living in regret and saying, "I wish I would've, and I wish I should've." To take a Tim Ferriss work-week term, the delayed life plan is really foolish, because you never know if you delayed it too long, and ultimately life as you know it can be stripped from you. To be really candid and authentic, I think that's a story that I have to share because I don't want anyone that can learn from those experiences, and the hardships that we've been through in the last couple years – if they can learn from that and not have to experience firsthand and some shapes and time and energy off the learning curve, then that's the story that I might feel obligated to share.

Colin: That sends chills down my back here, hearing that story. My mother-in-law, Friday, was having chest pains, went into the hospital, had a stent put in. Right now as we speak, she's in ICU. She went home, they discharged her, she was home for a couple days,

Afterword

and had some more chest pains yesterday. Went back into the hospital, and she's having some blood clotting issues, so she's in ICU right now, doing well. Doing well. She's stable, they say. They put her on a blood thinner, and it's looking good. You just never know. Yeah, I had a talk with my father the other day, and he gave me the same speech. It was kind of like, "Enjoy life. Don't get too caught up in the work, the work will be there tomorrow."

David: Yeah, it's amazing how our priorities get shifted. I'm pretty committed to my goals and self-work, but life will lead you astray, and you'll get distracted, so I think it's always important to know what your purpose is, what your mission is. If we should live to be old and tired and 90 years old in the rocking chair, making sure that those grandkids, those great-grandkids are gathered around the rocking chair that you're not telling them a story of "don't do what I did." Tell them a hell of a story that really inspires them.

I think there's a legacy piece there too. Sometimes I feel invincible, and I'm the host of "The Relentless Dentist" podcast, but you realize how fragile life can be. One person running a stoplight and hitting your family in a car, or a freak accident, or a condition, stroke will have you. Life as you know it can change in an instant. There's no reason to do things that you resent doing, so you spend most of your energy I think in service, but also playing the strength and enjoying the people that you work with, because you spend a lot of time with them. Especially the people that you get to come home to at the end of the day.

Colin: Have you been back overseas since you moved out there?

David: No, I made a promise to myself when we left, that we'd be back to Europe every year. I'm owed for eight, owed for nine. Now that Ben is old enough, and he's learning about some of these geographic things in Montessori school, we're trying to expand his world. What, we started with Mexico, and this spring we're going to Jamaica. As he gets older, and more in tuned with what we're saying, I intend to make sure that his passport's full of those stamps that we collected when we were traveling about Europe a decade or so ago.

Colin: Don't be like me and lose the passport that you had all the stamps in. I wish I could find it, it's somewhere. It wasn't lost, but I can't find my old passport for anything. I wish I could.

David: I gotcha.

Colin: We took our first family vacation in two and a half years last month. We went down, my wife and I, my 2-and-a-half-year-old boy, and my 3-month-old girl at the time, a month later, she's now 4 months. We went down to Clearwater Beach for a week, and it was a lot of fun. Found out my boy loves the sand, we had all these great events planned, all these fun things we were going to do, and we just couldn't drag him off the beach.

David: Yeah, it's amazing how children bring you back to the simplicity of life. And how important just some of those basic things are.

Colin: Yup, yup. No kidding, no kidding. Well, this has been a great conversation, I really appreciate your time. Is there any takeaways that you would give to somebody listening? What would be your 50 words of advice to any dentist listening to this today?

David: Oh, boy. It's hard to keep it in size. I would say most limiting factor is fear, that one of my favorite quotes, and I'm probably not going to hit this on the button of quota, but you get the understanding of it. But it's by Joseph Campbell, I learned from a book called *The Flinch*, about the power of doing the things you fear, and the quote is, "In the cave you most fear to enter lies the treasure that you seek." And I think as dentists, we live in a world where we think everything has to be perfect – crown margins. We go to dental school, and good enough isn't good enough, so you've got to go back and reset those denture teeth. We live in a world of near-perfection, and I'm not undermining that all. Clinical perfection is something that we should always strive for, but I think that keeps us fearbound. What's the patient going to say? Why are they sensitive after I've done the root canal, or the crown?

All those sorts of things have us a lot of times living in fear, and then you pick up a trade journal, and they talk about government

Afterword

involvement, and corporate dentistry, and lawsuits, and litigation, and HIPAA violation – I think it's easy to really start closing in and start playing it careful.

I think that's not how humans are supposed to do it. I think living a life in permanent beta where you're kind of testing, and exploring, and traveling, and picking up new techniques, and adding to the life that you had, and some of those are going to end up in mistakes. I'm way over 50 words here, but if I were going to give the most short advice, it's do those things you fear, and cherish the people that you love. I think our training had led us directly opposite of that, but what we've learned to get into dental school, and get out of dental school. If you follow that exactly as you've been coached, you'll lead a life of regret.

Cherish every moment, don't live a life of regret, and do the things you fear. If I could put a bow on it, it would be the things that I would stress in. I'm not an expert in that, it's stuff that I'm still bumping into walls, and forgetting, and getting distracted by. In my 40 years, if I could package something and give it to my son, that would be the message that I would send him.

Colin: Awesome, awesome. You've got your "Relentless Dentist" podcasts, and you've interviewed some awesome people on that, from Chris Griffin, Bruce Baird, Howard Farran, Woody, Chris Bowman – I'm going off the top of my head. If people want to hear more from you, how can they get in touch with you, or how can they get your podcast?

David: Well, I'd invite them to check that out, because there's 24 hours of free knowledge there, and it's not my knowledge. It's people who are generous enough to share, and I think if I could throw another word of advice, it's to stand on the shoulder of giants, and those are all giants to me. I learned a lot from those interviews, and I'm happy to share, because I think too often as dentists, we feel like we're on an island. I think that's the future, this podcasting free knowledge and when people are generous enough to share, you should be wise enough to accept that. I just think that life or practice is trial and error. I encourage people to subscribe to "Relentless Dentist" on iTunes. We have a website, RelentlessDentist.com, and one of the things that I really enjoy is hearing from listeners who have gained, and a lot of them are really in their career, even some of them still in dental school.

If someone has questions about just about anything, about how to prepare themselves best for a career in private practice, how to hire, how to fire, all those things that are typically learned from the school of hard knocks, I get emails all the time, so if someone wants to reach out to me, the e-mail that I use most often is David@VailValleyDentist.com, and sometimes those e-mails turn into phone calls, and I haven't monetized that podcast at all. It's just a labor of love. People are willing to dialogue about what they're hearing on there, I'm also happy to give them my time. It's become, like I said, a labor of love, and a passion, and I don't know what will become of it, but when you see a global medium growing exponentially in downloads – I think the fourth most downloaded country right now for a podcast is United Arab Emirates – you realize the impact that we can make by all sharing our, not only our successes but also our challenges. So that's what "The Relentless Dentist" is all about.

Colin: How many episodes are you up to right now?

David: We're well over 50, I think we're about to release maybe number 54 or 55 this weekend. I have visions of making a true weekly podcast, but sometimes practice demands and family demands take precedent. As I see the podcast grow, I get more and more motivated to continue to turn out excellent content for the listeners.

Colin: Awesome, awesome. I suggest anybody, I think it's the RelentlessDentist.com. Isn't that a shortcut to get to it?

David: Absolutely.

Colin: Awesome, awesome. Well, hey, I really appreciate you being on here, Dr. Dave. Any last remarks or comments?

David: You know, I think if I were to say one of the life hacks that someone taught me a long time ago is, you are the five people that you spend the most time with.

Colin: Like that Warren Buffett quote.

David: Yeah. I've seen it in different iterations from different people, but it's really true. I think in a nontech world, that was the people you've lived with and worked with. You don't want to think about firing your family and firing your friends. So if you want to reach a higher level, I think surrounding yourself with information that's available through these podcasts, it's readily available. Colin shares it, we have a mutual friend, David Phelps, that's now sharing it. You don't have to live a life of commodity when people are willing to share their bold moves. I think just constantly taking positive input because when you're surrounded by information of beheadings and plane crashes, it's easy to shift your mind in a negative way, but there's lots out there that you can combat that with, and the five people that you spend the most time with, they can be in a virtual world now. To me that's the beauty of the podcasting realm that you and I share.

Colin: Awesome, yeah. I can't agree more, it's a crazy world out there. Half the people you meet today will be crazier than average.

David: That's right.

Colin: Well, cool. Hey, I appreciate your time so much, and I look forward to our next conversation, whenever that may be.

David: Yeah, I love that. Yeah, thank you so much for having me on.

Colin: Take care.

David: You as well.

Now, I can't always come up with the ideas, I'm not skilled enough, so sometimes I have to outsource or pick people's brains or see it already done. I had seen it done through your work and I knew it was good, quality work.

Probably the thing that is most important to me, if I'm sending my son to a doctor, I want him to see a pediatrician. If my son has a severe eye problem, I want him to see a pediatric ophthalmologist.

So I feel that that specialized knowledge is so valuable, and knowing that you had a background in dentistry, not as a student but actually growing up in the industry, that's stuff you can't teach.

– Dr. David Maloley
COLORADO

They're Coming

The Four Horsemen of Dentistry are on the move. Now that you've read this book, you know that. You might not agree with every detail of my analysis, but if you're keeping a close eye on the dental industry, you're aware that it's only a matter of time.

In fact, time – or rather, timing – is the issue. Three of the Horsemen are already here, and that's more than enough challenge for most dental practices. But when the Fourth Horseman gets here, there will be almost no time to react. The Great Recession taught us that. But if that's not enough to convince you, look at the run on the banks that happened in the early days of the Great Depression.

You can keep doing what you're doing by chasing patients through advertising. You can even step up your efforts to grow your patient base using the same tired, obsolete approach to dental marketing.

From the longer perspective, that's equivalent to rearranging deck chairs on the *Titanic*. If you find some comfort in ritual gestures, by all means, go ahead. But it won't save you in the long run.

It's better to be proactive to secure your practice's future against the powerful forces facing dentists. You've seen the answer to the coming dental apocalypse. The only question now is whether you'll accept it in time.

As I noted before, what we offer isn't for everyone. But if you're a dentist who wants to be able to thumb his or her nose at the Four Horsemen of Dentistry, go to smartboxwebmarketing.com/blueprint and schedule a **Patient Attraction System Blueprint™ Session.**

We reserve these sessions for **serious** dentists who want to see a patient attraction system that can **double their practice.** You can get more patients, **more profits, and more freedom.**

And you can tell the Horsemen to **kiss off.**

Remember – **no more sleepless nights.**

If you're not working towards something that's going to give you freedom, what in the world are you working towards?

I'll tell you: MORE WORK. There's a better way. You just need the blueprint to build it.

– Dr. Michael Abernathy
FOUNDER, SUMMIT PRACTICE SOLUTIONS

There's no time to waste!

For a blueprint on how to defend yourself from the Four Horsemen of Dentistry, call **888.741.1413** or go to **www.DefeatThe4Horsemen.com**

Appendix
ADDITIONAL PATIENT ATTRACTION RESOURCES

Dental Marketing Mistakes

I know from experience that SmartBox isn't the right choice for all dentists, and vice versa. But this is my profession, and it irks me when I hear dentists talk about the extravagant promises and incredibly poor results they got from their previous marketing firms.

This SmartBox blog post is from June 2016. There's no "magic bullet," as much as some marketing firms – that may or may not specialize in dentistry – would like you to believe. Don't fall for marketing double-talk.

Bright, Shiny Dental Objects

To the layperson, dental terminology and processes are basically incomprehensible.

That's why we encourage our dentists to talk at their patients' level when discussing dental problems and solutions.

To the vast majority of dentists, marketing terminology and processes are basically incomprehensible. That may sound harsh, but our extensive experience helping dentists get more and better patients has confirmed it. The reason that too many dentists don't understand marketing is that there are a huge number of marketing firms out there who "explain" how they're going to help you succeed without actually explaining anything.

They toss out phrases like "innovative approach," "state-of-the-art algorithms," "optimized search engine results," or "segmented market stratification" at dizzying speed. If you ask for clarification, you get a highly technical-sounding "explanation" that leaves you thinking that maybe you should just let them get on with helping you, because you don't understand this at all.

Those hyped-up claims are the "bright, shiny objects" of dental marketing, and too many dentists fall for them.

If you've been reading this blog for any length of time, or following our podcasts, you know that we don't believe in bright, shiny objects. There's no **single** technique or marketing "innovation" that's a guaranteed ticket to success. If there were, that single approach would be the **only** thing that **every** dentist would use.

What we do believe in and offer our dentists is a proven system of attracting **more and better patients.** The parts and pieces of our **Patient Attraction System™** are easy to understand and fit logically together to make your marketing work 24/7 to position you as the **only** logical choice to solve patients' dental problems.

I firmly believe that if you don't understand **everything** about what we're doing for you and **how** each part will help achieve your end goal, then we haven't done our job correctly.

Here's how our system works.

1. We focus your marketing strongly on your online presence because the vast majority of people find dentists online these days.
2. We help you differentiate yourself from your competitors so that you can stand out in a crowded marketplace.
3. We help you give prospective patients reasons to like and trust you.

4. We help you stay in front of patients until they're ready to choose you to solve their dental problems.

5. We drive prospective patients to your website and fine-tune your site to answer their questions and get them to pick up the phone.

6. We help you automatically track each and every new patient call that comes into your office so that you can see what parts of your marketing are working and what needs to be altered.

7. We alert you to staff phone etiquette problems that may be costing you new patient conversions.

8. Over time, all of those efforts help you get more patients, more profits, and more freedom.

When it comes to the technical aspects of how we do what we do for our dentists, you can find plain-language explanations in this blog, in the Patient Attraction Podcast™, in our stunning Patient Attraction Magazine™, and on our website. Search engine optimization, Zetetics® phone tracking, drip marketing, dental videos, and much, much more are explained in detail.

In fact, we basically give away the store – you can find all the information you need to set up your own patient attraction system **without** us.

Don't fall for the bright, shiny dental marketing objects. They don't last, and they won't get you where you want to go.

"I Find Your Lack of Integration ... Disturbing."

You don't always get what you pay for with a dental marketing firm.

I'm always astonished by how many dentists hear what they want to hear when it comes to marketing. The marketing firm you use – or that you're thinking of using – may be selling you a technique that isn't going to help you attain the one result that really matters.

I addressed that issue in this podcast from January 2017.

Patient Attraction Episode 977
Your Major Dental Marketing Challenge

Most dentists have been sold a bill of goods when it comes to their marketing. You're promised things that are supposed to solve your problems for getting new patients. But your **sole** marketing challenge is to put more new patients in your chairs. After the break, I'll tell you why mistaking the **means** to an end for the end itself is a really bad idea.

Thanks for watching the Patient Attraction Podcast™. I'm Colin Receveur.

I'm the son of a very successful dentist in the greater Louisville, Kentucky, area. Plus, I know a **lot** of dentists, and I've learned a few things about them.

Most dentists are good tacticians, but lousy strategists. When it comes to planning and executing the steps needed to reach a desired clinical outcome, they're excellent. But that tactical ability usually doesn't carry over into their dental marketing.

There's often a disconnect between the various parts of their marketing so that they don't work to reinforce each other. Then along comes some marketer who says that **this widget** will make everything work just fine.

Unfortunately, the widget isn't designed to harmonize your marketing, and the results are mixed at best. That widget is just another marketing tactic.

It doesn't matter whether it's SEO, an outdoor campaign, an email automation system, or anything else. It's one more **means** to an end that won't get you to where you want to go.

Your major marketing challenge, and your single marketing goal, is to put **more new patients** in your chairs. Ideally, they'd also be **better** patients with higher average case values. **That's** how you make money, not by increased engagement, higher Google page ranking, or more Facebook "likes." Those are tactics, and they should never be mistaken for an integrated strategy.

If your goal is to attract more and better patients, you need a system that makes every part of your marketing reinforce the others. And you can discover the power of a proven, integrated system in just one step.

Go to www.smartboxwebmarketing.com/blueprint and schedule a **Patient Attraction System Blueprint™ Session.** They are reserved only for **serious** dentists who want to see a patient attraction system that can **double their practice.** You can get **more patients, more profits, and more freedom.**

And the patient attraction system is backed by our industry-leading **$10K Guarantee™.**

Join me for our next podcast. Until tomorrow, keep moving forward.

Dental Half-Marketing

It's tough enough out there for dental practices. Few dentists can afford to waste their hard-earned marketing dollars with a marketing company that doesn't deliver a full solution. Here's what you need to watch out for.

Patient Attraction Episode 920
The 5 Scams of Dental Marketing

What is your dental marketing company doing for you? If they're providing SEO services, pay-per-click services, and/or video for your website, you need to make sure that they're looking at the big picture. If they're not, you're throwing money away on what are essentially marketing scams. I'll be right back to tell you how to protect yourself. Stay tuned.

I'm Colin Receveur, and welcome to the Patient Attraction Podcast™.

I'm really irritated right now, and I hope you'll bear with me. I've been talking with dentists about their web marketing and their current marketing providers. Those marketing companies are basically polishing turds, as the saying goes, and serving them up as bright and shiny marketing solutions.

And without pointing fingers at any particular company, those dentists are being scammed, in my opinion.

Scam number 1: Say you're a new dentist who doesn't have a website yet. Your marketing firm says they're going to optimize your marketing for local search. That flat doesn't work, because your website is what you need to show up on local search.

Scam number 2: You do have a website, and they're optimizing it. But you have dated, low-quality content on the site, as far as Google is concerned. You're throwing away money, because you still won't place high in search results.

Scam number 3: If you're paying a company for PPC and they're not focused on improving your website's Quality score, you're paying too much. Your Quality score majorly affects your cost for PPC.

Scam number 4: Does your marketing company do your doctor and patient videos? If those videos aren't optimized for Google, you're not getting everything you're paying for.

And scam number 5: Exactly what are those companies providing for you? Impressions, hits, clicks, click-throughs, likes, follows? Those are great but they won't make you a dime. The only metric that counts is new patient calls to your practice. Everything else is just a means to that end.

Online dental marketing is a complex process in which everything has to work together to get you the results you want. If your current dental marketing company isn't looking at the overall online picture and taking the appropriate steps, you're being scammed.

Join me for tomorrow's podcast. Until then, keep moving forward.

That Is Seriously Lame

The success rate for dental practices is over 99 percent. There are times when that fact just amazes me. I know that practice management, and particularly marketing, aren't covered in dental school. But there are some common-sense things that just seem to elude a lot of dentists.

Sometimes, you just have to get blunt. This podcast was one of those times.

Patient Attraction Episode 930
Dentists' Excuses for Lack of Success

SmartBox works with more than 550 dentists on three continents to help them attract more and better patients. I know a LOT of other dentists besides our clients. I've heard every excuse in the book, and more, for their lack of success. When we come back, I'll run down some of the top excuses and tell you what to do instead.

I'm Colin Receveur, founder and CEO of SmartBox. Thanks for watching the Patient Attraction Podcast™.

I'm the son of a very successful dentist in the greater Louisville, Kentucky, area.

I guess I kind of have a soft spot for dentists, and I want them all to succeed. But I've known way too many dentists who were doomed right out of the gate because they made excuses for their lack of success.

I'm going to run down some of the lamest and most powerful excuses I've heard.

Excuse number 1: I'm not trained in marketing.

Well, excuse me, but DUH! Dentists don't get training in marketing in dental school, so why are you trying to handle it yourself? Would you hire you to handle someone else's marketing?

Excuse number 2: I thought our marketing was working.

You THOUGHT, you didn't KNOW? How many new patients did you get each month? What was your average case value for those patients? How much did you spend on your marketing? It's pretty darned easy to tell whether your marketing is attracting the patients you want and need.

Excuse number 3: All patients care about are price and insurance.

No, those are just the patients that your marketing is attracting. What are you doing to attract patients who will pay more for a dentist they trust?

And number 4: I can't afford to be undercut by my competitors.

See the answer to excuse number 3: You're attracting the wrong kinds of patients. You can't afford to engage in a race to the bottom.

Are you ready to stop making excuses?

Are you ready to fast-track your success?

If you answered "yes," go to www.smartboxwebmarketing.com/blueprint and schedule a Patient Attraction System Blueprint™ Session. They are free to serious dentists who want to see a patient attraction system that can double their practice. You can get more patients, more profits, and more freedom.

Join me for our next podcast. Until tomorrow, keep moving forward.

The Patient Attraction System™: A Quick Overview

The following interview between Dr. Woody Oakes and me includes an overview of the elements of the **Patient Attraction System™.** I decided to include it as a quick reference. Keep in mind, though, that this interview is from November 2014. The internet marches on, and in some respects it's the fastest-evolving organism on the planet. The broad outlines are here, but some of the specifics about how to implement different aspects have changed.

The key takeaway is that if you want to crush your competition with web marketing, you're looking at doing a tremendous amount of work that doesn't directly make you a dime. It just gets you more patients to make money on.

"How To Crush the Competition with Web Marketing" with Colin Receveur & Dr. Woody Oakes

Woody: Good evening, everybody. This is Woody. And tonight it's my pleasure to be with you and our guest, Colin Receveur with SmartBox Marketing. Colin, how are you doing this evening?

Colin: Doing well. How are you, Dr. Oakes?

Woody: Doing good. I enjoyed your cover on the issue of "The Profitable Dentist" as Superman.

Colin: Well, that's what we try to be is a superhero for our dentists that we work with.

Woody: You are built exactly like that, right?

Colin: Exactly like it, muscles and all.

Woody: Well, I envy you then. That's quite a cover. I thought it turned out well.

Colin: I did as well.

Woody: I read it before, but this morning I looked at the magazine and reread the interview we did. Anybody who is on the call tonight who hasn't gotten that particular issue of the magazine with Colin in his Superman outfit on the cover needs to read that little three-page interview. I think it will be really informative to you.

Colin, one of the first things I want to talk about, because you do so many things, SmartBox Marketing is not just another website design company. As people will learn in the interview, you do tracking, you do video. I mean just dozens and dozens of things that we're going to be talking about. One of the first things I wanted to talk about that kind of differentiates your company from other companies is something you call the mirror effect. Can you kind of tell our listeners tonight what exactly that is?

Colin: The mirror effect is all about what kind of patients you really want to attract. Let me give you an example. I talked to a prospective dentist earlier this morning who had called in, and one of his big complaints with his website was he was getting all the patients that were coming in looking for discounts and coupons, and they were price shopping for the cheapest service provider.

When I went and looked at his website, his website was full of discounts and coupons and free everything. The mirror effect is when your patients are out there looking, when your prospective patients are searching for a service provider, when they look at your website, they see themselves in the reflection. If you put out there that you have the best prices in town, and coupons, and discounts, and free everything, that's going to be the type of person you attract. They are going to see themselves reflected in your website or in your marketing.

If you put on your website that you have the best service in town and you provide tremendous value, not necessarily the cheapest price, then the patients that are looking for a higher level of service, a higher level of care are going to see their reflection in that website, and they're going to choose a service provider that fits the model that they're looking for.

Woody: That's a good point, because oftentimes a website company will talk about, "We get 150 new patients a month," or, "We get 200 new patients a month." Oftentimes, that's kind of a misnomer because what kind of patients are you getting? Are you getting the shoppers? Kind of a good example, or maybe a good analogy, is kind of like dating, for example. If you are a 4 and you are trying to attract 10s, it's probably not going to work. If you want to attract 9s and 10s, then you probably should get yourself as close as you can to 9 or 10. Kind of the same thing with a website. The way the website looks, performs, functions, the message it sends is kind of what you are going to get back. If you throw up one of the discount websites like we see in *Dental Economics* and some of the trade journals, then you are going to get a certain type of patient back. It's not going to be the quality that you might want. Whereas, if you are giving an image of value and it just shows from the website that, "Hey, I'm not the cheapest in town, but we are pretty daggone good, and you are going to receive high value."

Colin, one thing I wanted to talk about, and we might be getting ahead of ourselves a little bit, I wanted to talk about your father, who is a dentist. I think one of the best dentists in town. I think I've told you before one of the three dentists in town I would actually let ... well, one of the two dentists in town I would let touch my own mouth. One of them just retired. Tell us a little bit about how SmartBox got started. We might be going backwards a little bit, but growing up in a dental family and seeing your dad and the high quality of dentistry that he does, how did you get started with SmartBox?

Colin: Well, I guess it was just kind of my generation. I remember back as far as I can remember I was kind of tinkering around on the internet and building web pages back when I was in grade school. I remember my mom screaming and yelling, wanting me to go outside or get off the computer, and all I wanted to do was build web pages, play on the internet, and build things online rather than building things out in the driveway.

My dad's idea of day care growing up was I would get off school and come to the office and file charts. So I guess it was just kind of the merging of two worlds. I always enjoyed the web design aspect, being online, marketing, and having Dr. Ron as a father, being a dentist, growing up in his office and learning from the ground up what drives a dental practice not just in the front office but also in the backend: marketing, how he positioned himself to attract patients. Now we run all of his marketing campaigns for him. We have for the past six or seven years now exclusively.

Woody: Yeah. And Ron is not paying me to say this, but he's known as one of the high-end dentists in town, known as somebody, if you really want quality, this is where you go to. But he's also known as being a little bit more expensive than the other dentists in town. But that combination that we talked about of value with high-quality dentistry. So, do you think that's where you kind of got this concept of "Let's market for a certain kind of patient, but let's market for the kind that my dad, or Ron, would want"?

Colin: It is. Well, with any marketing you have to find a way to differentiate yourself. When that consumer is out there looking on the internet or looking in the Yellow Pages – if anybody actually still uses that – wherever they are looking, that consumer is trying to choose who's going to be their dentist. There has to be something that makes you stand out from the crowd, either the best price, or the best service, or the best value, or that you are the most pain-free dentist in town. There has to be something that that consumer can chew on, can bite into, and say, "This is my guy. This is the guy I'm going to choose to be my dentist." Because, you know, dentistry is a personal thing. It's not a plumber. It's somebody that's working in your mouth. It's not something that a consumer does one search on Google and goes, "OK, this guy looks good. I'm going to go to him."

So yeah, there has to be a way to differentiate yourself. If you don't want the price shoppers and the bargain shoppers, what do you do? Well, you go towards value. You go towards offering great service, and great results, and a very high level of service and product, which is the direction that Ron went. You might know better than I do. I know of one other dentist in town that has a Galileos CT scan machine in his office. So when he is doing reconstructions and implants, they don't have to go to the hospital. They can get it all done in one place.

As far as dentists that are actually placing implants and restoring them in the Louisville market area, how many dentists are doing that? There's the one guy out on Dixie Highway that does only mini implants. There's a couple of periodontists around town that will place the implants but they won't do the restorative. So he's positioned himself in the market as the go-to guy, all in one place, the expert, so to speak, for the Louisville market. That's what differentiates him.

That's what we want to help dentists do, is to find your niche in the market. Maybe that's not it, the way Ron has gone, but there is a way to differentiate every practice to make them more appealing to the consumers.

Woody: Another point that a lot of dentists don't know, or maybe they know it and don't really think about that much, most of the really good dentists I know have multiple websites. I don't know how many Ron has now. Probably, what, four, five, or six?

Colin: He had actually 12 up until a few months ago, and we went in reverse and we merged them down into four or five, which he has now.

Woody: A lot of dentists have one website and they wonder, "How come I'm not getting any implants?" Here's a dentist that has one website devoted just to implants that eventually directs traffic to his website. So there's a whole lot more to it than most dentists realize. Colin, the next thing I want to talk about is dominating the first page of Google, why it's so critical. Everybody has heard that you need to be on the first page of Google. A lot of people have heard that you need to be number 1 on the first page of Google. So let's talk about that a little bit. I think everybody knows what Google is, but let's talk about getting on the first page of Google, what ranking really counts, some of the things you need to know about that.

Colin: There was a study done a few years ago by a large – kind of like the Nielsen of the internet – a large statistical company that found that if you are not in the top three search results, you are simply not really going to be found. The number 1 search result is taking roughly 50 percent of the clicks; the number 2 result, 25 percent; and the number 3, 15 percent to 16 percent. By the time you get back to number 4 to number 10, you are splitting that amongst a market share of 10 percent to 15 percent of the overall searches on that term.

Now, that study came out in '07 and '08, and things have changed a lot since then. The search results have become a lot more intertwined, a lot more complex. If you go right now to Google and search for "your town dentist" or "your town implant dentist" or "your town Invisalign," you are going to see all kinds of different search engines within Google. You are going to see their AdWords, their pay-per-click engine, which is going to come in on the side or the top. You are going to see the local search engine, which is the maps and the addresses. You are going to see the organic search engine, which is the traditional area in the middle bottom.

They also have YouTube videos that they are now showing right on the first page of Google. And then they also have their latest search engine, Google AdWords Express, which is a pay-per-click advertisement, but if you go search and you see that some of the pay-per-click advertisements have two or three lines and others have six, seven, or eight lines, it's the same cost in most cases, but Google is allowing you to have a bigger ad on the front page. So when a consumer is on there searching, dominating the search engines simply means that you are going to be found in multiple positions.

The old days of having a website that has one position ranking … you know, you have a website listed in the organic results, and maybe it's number 1, and that's great. But in today's Google, you have search results that are all around you – below you, above you, to the left, to the right. Dominating the search engines means that your patients can find you everywhere. You have a pay-per-click ad that's running. You have a local search page that's been optimized and you are showing up, an organic search page. You have some

YouTube videos that we've optimized and are showing up right there on the first page. It goes back to the old branding. The more times your consumers see you and hear your name, the more you are recognized and the more comfortable they are moving towards calling you, making an appointment, and becoming a patient.

Woody: And Colin, if you are like on the third page of Google, what are your chances of somebody calling you?

Colin: Oh, I would say zero, but there's always that one in a million chance, I think.

Woody: Right. And I'll tell you one thing I've noticed, because I did some research before this interview, and looking at your dad's practice, I mean he's just all over the place. You do all these different searches and his practice pops up all over the place. So you've obviously done an excellent job of putting him everywhere.

Colin: That's what it's all about. He pulls in 15-20 large cases, you know, the implant-specific types of patients that he's looking for, the internet is sending him 15-20 new patients a month with everything that we're doing online.

Woody: One of the things we talk about is getting in front of your "tribe." Tribe is simply a term for your followers. In other words, at "The Profitable Dentist," we have maybe 25,000 dentists who are in our tribe that follow us, get our magazine, and so on. So what are some ways of keeping your name as a dentist in front of your tribe? How do you do that?

Colin: There's all kinds of ways. A lot of dentists are doing newsletters. And that's a fantastic way to reach out and touch people. Make sure that you are putting some kind of compelling content in the newsletter. I've seen some pretty bland ones come out that I'm not sure patients even open. But newsletters are a very traditional way of staying in front of people. Going online, we have automatic communication systems called auto responders. We partnered up with Infusionsoft® to offer a phenomenal auto-responder system that you can reach out and automatically stay in front of your patients for two or three years after they've visited your website.

Woody: You think about an auto responder as simply technology that does what we used to do by hand, and the sheer numbers are just incredible when you think a person goes to your website, maybe they order a free report, and then they are in that sales funnel for two or three years without you doing anything. It's all done by the software and, in your case, Infusionsoft.

Colin: We've had dentists come to us and they've had these spreadsheets that they have one of their front office staff ... you know, they have columns: Send direct mail piece one. Send direct mail piece two. Send email three or A, B, C. And they have these huge spreadsheets that they are using to track every patient and what marketing piece they're received. They're dedicating tremendous resources in terms of labor to this. It's something that we can literally automate for pennies per marketing piece that goes out.

If you have 100 prospects that opt in on your website in a month and each of those prospects is going to get 30 pieces of information, whether it be an email or a postcard in the mail, or a text message, they get 30 pieces over the next two years and you've got 100 a month, you are at 2,400 contacts over two years times 30 pieces apiece is 72,000 pieces of information that you've sent out over a two-year period. To do that without technology and automation, you could have a whole team of people working on that. And we can automate that.

Woody: It would be totally impossible if you think about it. Colin, the other thing is, once you are sending out all this information to people who have kind of raised their hand that they have an interest in your practice, and they click on to your website or they make some move in a positive manner, how do you convert those clicks to phone calls?

Colin: You have to give them a reason. You have to answer their question and tell them why you are the best person for their needs. The general rule is when somebody comes to your website, you want to talk 70 percent about how you can help them and 30 percent about who you are.

We do these Swift Kick web critiques where I get on their website, and kind of like when you are watching the Super Bowl on TV, you've got the guy with the marker drawing the plays on the screen and showing you what's going on, we do this for prospective clients and show them what's going on with their web marketing. When we're going through these videos with clients, we show them, "Hey, here's what's missing. Here's the piece that is why you are not getting patients to call you." We go on their website and they are talking about how great they are, and they have a list of everything they do clinically. Or we go on their website and they've got pictures of implant surgeries and flapping gums and all kinds of stuff that patients don't want to see.

It's like when you go to the mechanic. You don't want to see pictures of how they change your head gasket or fix your transmission. You just want to know it's going to drive when you pull it out. That's the same thing patients want. They just want to know that you are the guy to fix it, you are not going to hurt them, and you are going to do a good job.

Woody: I continue to be amazed at people who put periodontal surgery on the home page of their website. I mean, all the blood, guts, and glory there and somehow they think that's going to attract patients. It's just incredible. Colin, another thing I wanted to ask you about is actually quantifying your results and something you call Zetetics® phone tracking. Can you explain what that means, how it works?

Colin: Well, Zetetics, by definition, is the quantification of something that's unknown; it's an algebraic term. So we named our new patient phone tracking system after it because that seemed appropriate. So many dentists do marketing, or they have a website, or they are spending money out there in any marketing field, whether it's billboard, radio, TV, newspaper, the internet, pay-per-click, SEO, local search, and they're spending money every month cranking out these marketing campaigns. And when I ask them, "How many patients did that send you last month? How many dollars did that generate?" they stutter. They don't know the answer.

So that's the basis of what Zetetics does, is we can take any marketing campaign you are doing, put one of our trackable phone numbers in it, and this isn't just a phone tracking system. This isn't just something that we tell you, "Hey, you got 32 calls with this last month." This is a system that we can show you how many calls you got, how many cases you presented, how many dollars were generated. We record the calls for you that we can review them with your staff.

So the marketing funnel doesn't end when that phone rings. The marketing funnel ends when they write you the check. And we want to make sure that with our dentist clients, the ball doesn't get dropped as that patient moves through the funnel from the search, to the website, to the auto responders, to actually picking up the phone and calling once they've developed that level of trust. Passing them off to the front desk, we want to make sure that that transition is there. Because otherwise, again, the dentist is spending money, money, money going out, nothing is coming back in.

Woody: And again, you can track all that basically automatically?

Colin: All done for you.

Woody: That's incredible. When I think about how it used to be done and all the man and woman hours taken to do that, to know that this all can be done this way now is totally incredible. Another point I want to make as we go through the interview, a lot of dentists think that they can practice dentistry plus keep up on all the internet stuff, too. I'll tell you as somebody who has tried real hard, you can't do it. There is way too much going on out there. That's why you need to bring in an expert like Colin who literally has been doing this since grade school and keeps up on this all the time.

Your main goal is to be a dentist, to be productive. You are the most productive when the bur is on the tooth or you are doing implants, doing grafts, whatever. It's not trying to learn the latest and greatest about the internet. So if you learn nothing else from this teleseminar tonight, learn the fact that you cannot do this. You have to have somebody who does this all day long to be successful.

Colin, the next thing I wanted to talk to you about was how to optimize videos to be number 1 on Google. One of the things that happens sometimes is people will do a search for "dentist" in, say, New Albany, Indiana. They might pull up two or three websites. They look at the websites and then they make a decision based on that website – which one or two they are going to call. Oftentimes, or the way it used to be is that, say a dentist had a video of testimonials that would be very engaging. I would watch one video and say, "That's kind of interesting." And then you are kind of drawn into it and you watch another one. And then you watch another one. And after hearing the social proof of two or three people talking about how great this dentist is, then you are tempted to call. I remember a video that your dad had a number of years ago where he talked about the reason he got into dentistry, and it was very, very compelling. I think one of the first dentists in our area to do a video. Talk a little bit about how you can optimize videos to be number 1 on Google.

Colin: Google, in many markets, is putting videos right there on the first page. Sometimes at the top, sometimes at the bottom. It depends on how well optimized your videos are. Just like your website, we can promote your videos organically right up to the first page.

You hit a number of killer points, Woody. Videos humanize you. Every dentist in today's market, I can look in any market area in any state of this country and I will find 10 dentists that are "painless" and "cosmetic." And if that is the niche, if that's your niche, there's nothing wrong with that. I have a lot of dentist clients that are extremely successful with those two keywords. But you have to find a way to, again, set yourself apart from every other dentist that's a cosmetic dentist and everybody else that does painless dentistry. No matter how many times you say you are the most painless dentist in town or you have the best cosmetic results in town, there is absolutely no way you can put into words what a video can do on your website. For instance, just like you said, Dr. Ron talking about how he got into it, his passion. Or you put a patient in front of the camera that never smiled at family events before, so they always had their hand in front of their mouth because they were so embarrassed. You put that person in front of a camera.

When we're doing interviews with patients, the camera is sitting off to the side. This isn't a process where we stick the camera in their face and tell them what to say. It's a process that we want to evoke emotion out of it. And it's a conversation that we have out of it, and the video camera is just running on the side. When that patient goes on camera and says, "He changed my life with these implants, or these veneers, or this partial he made for me, or he was able to fix my denture so I could eat comfortably again," whatever it is, it goes back to that mirror effect – you are going to attract patients that that message resonates with. When they see your patient testimonials that talk about how you, as a dentist, changed their life, you are going to attract more of those kind of patients.

Woody: You are right about kind of the quality of the video. I've watched a lot of these. When they start out, the patient is obviously kind of nervous because they are on camera. But after the first 30 seconds they relax, forget about the camera, and it's kind of like they are just talking to you. That's the part that is really powerful. That's the social proof that everybody needs to pick up the phone and call that office.

Colin: And something else that should be said is I see a lot of dentists these days doing their own video. They buy a flip cam. I think that's fantastic. I think there is definitely a place and a purpose for that. But what you don't see on a lot of the videos we produce is, you know, you see the person with the emotion spilling out. We did a video shoot up in New Jersey last month, and one of the ladies had a young daughter that had just died of cancer. This dentist – honest to God, true story – this dentist had gone out of his office with his front staff and helped carry this little 6-year-old girl with cancer up the stairs and into their office to do dentistry on her. I don't know. I'm going to be a father here in a few months and that has …

Woody: Oh, congratulations. Didn't know that.

Colin: Oh yeah. January we are expecting our first. I don't know. I guess that kind of resonates differently with me with that perspective. This lady was on video, and at the time we were filming, her daughter had passed away from the cancer. All this emotion just … it was an hourlong interview that we edited down to three minutes. It was just incredible.

When you talk to somebody, you talk to them as a person, not as, "Here. Talk into my camera." The quality and the energy and the emotion that goes into stuff like that.

Woody: Yeah, it really comes through on a video. I mean you can't write copy that can even come close to really good video that's done well. Colin, one of the questions I wanted to ask you, too, and this is kind of an open-ended question, but what is it that makes SmartBox different from any other provider? Because there are a lot of providers in this niche.

Colin: There's a lot of web designers out there. And by web designer I mean somebody that is good at designing websites – the graphical aspect, the aesthetically pleasing aspect. There's a lot of companies out there that only do piecemeal marketing. They only do pay-per-click or they only do local search. They will give you this little one piece of the puzzle; one piece of the puzzle here and there.

The difference between us and those guys is we put the pieces together. We don't just design websites. We design beautiful websites, aesthetically pleasing websites, also with functionality in mind. I'll give you a perfect example. The two biggest things we see on dentists' websites these days that are killing their new patient flow, their results, is they are using Flash. Flash isn't compatible with Google. Flash isn't compatible with any Apple product. So if you have a patient on an iPad, an iPhone, an iPod trying to look at your website and you've got Flash on it, they can't see that. Google can't read Flash. So if you have a Flash website, Google is looking at your site and they're going, "What are these big holes everywhere?"

Or, "The whole website is missing." Well, it's a big Flash file.

And the second thing is, and these are extremely popular, the rotating banners on the front page where they have the pictures that scroll around in circles. We've done dozens of tests with those, studies, where we have taken out the scrolling pictures and put in an offer, such as "Get our free report" or just put in a static image that doesn't change. Every time we do it, the results go up. I can't read people's minds why a patient searches and they see that rotating banner and they don't call, click, or contact you. But I think people get kind of mesmerized by it. You have five or 10 images that rotate every five or 10 seconds and they just sit there and watch it and they don't do anything. So my guess is as good as yours on that.

Woody: Yeah. I've seen that. We had a couple years ago in our coaching program probably one of the highest producing dentists in the country, a guy out of Texas. His website had Flash and had that little rotating banner like you are talking about. We went back and forth about, "You got to get rid of that." He said, "Well, it looks good." I'm like, "Well, it looks good but it's killing you." To this day I think it's still up there.

Well, Colin, we're running out of time. By the way, fascinating interview. I learned a couple things I didn't know. Any time I learn something from an interview, I consider it worthwhile. Anybody on the call, how can they learn more? How can they get in touch with you? What are the next steps?

Colin: For anybody looking for more information, you can go check out www.BestDentalWebsites.com. And for anybody that is looking to find out more specifically about how we can help them, I'm going to extend an offer to anybody that's on this call tonight. We have our Swift Kick critiques where I personally spend 30-45 minutes developing a marketing plan. I talk about that Super Bowl marker, drawing on the screen, showing you what we can do to improve your web presence, how we can help you to find those new patients and attract them, get them to call your office. So for the first 10 people that respond to this call, you can go to www.DentalSwiftKick.com. They are regularly $250. But just fill out that form on the page and we're going to waive that $250 fee for the first 10 people that respond. There's no obligation, no commitment. If you decide you like our ideas and you can find somebody better that's a better fit for your needs, feel free to take it and run.

Woody: And Colin, any phone number if somebody would just like to call and bounce a few ideas off of you?

Colin: They can reach me at 888-741-1413.

Woody: Sounds good. Once again, thank you for a very informative evening. Again, congratulations on that new baby coming in January. Catch up on your sleep is the best advice I can give you.

Colin: Well, thank you. I appreciate your time, Dr. Oakes.

Woody: OK. Take care.

Dental Content and Content Marketing

Google, Dental Content, & Corporate Dentistry

Matt Tungate, SmartBox's Director of Production, joined me for the June 2016 episode of our Inside Patient Attraction™ webinar series.

It turns out that producing great content not only enhances your search engine results placement; it's also a great way to recruit and convert new dental prospects to appointed patients. And great dental content may be one of your best weapons to combat corporate dentistry.

Inside Patient Attraction™ June 2016

Colin: The rules for being found on Google are constantly evolving and changing. The dos from yesterday have become the do nots of today. We're going to talk a little bit today about how do you get found on Google, what's the biggest thing that you can use to motivate and compel Google to rank your website highly, right after the break.

Welcome back to a very special Inside Patient Attraction™. Today I'm joined here with Matt Tungate, our Director of Production here at SmartBox. Welcome on the show, Matt.

Matt: Glad to be here, man. Super excited to talk today.

Colin: Appreciate your time. Today, I want to talk about content marketing. With Google, Google is the big gorilla in the room right now. They've got, 98 percent of people go online to search. Now, somewhere around 75 percent to 80 percent of people go specifically to Google to search, and even more importantly, 75 percent to 80 percent of people are never going to look past the first page of search results. If your dental practice isn't found on the first page, you're wasting your money marketing online. Nobody is finding you.

Today I want to talk about the number one key most important thing that you need to be doing to get your website up at the top of Google's listings: and that is content marketing. Welcome on the show, Matt.

Matt: Yeah, super excited to be here.

Colin: Let's start off, Matt. First of all, what is good content? What makes up great content that Google likes to consume?

Matt: Content is anything you put on your website, whether that's writing – which we'll talk a lot about today – video, it could be graphics; it could be a lot of things that are meant to draw in and to educate the dental prospect.

Colin: Why does Google care about content?

Matt: Well, Google has always cared about content. Google is there to provide information that people want. Google succeeds when people want to go to Google because they know they can find what they want. Google is always looking to give you, the searcher or the dental prospect or whomever, the results that they want to find. That way, they keep using Google.

Colin: What is a searcher looking for? Why do you think a dental prospective patient goes to Google to search? What are they seeking?

Matt: That's a really good question. That's something that all dentists should ask themselves. The prospect is not there looking for the dentist. The prospect is not there looking for how that dentist might be the person that they want to go and see. The dental prospect is looking for a way to solve their problems. They don't care about anything else. What the prospect is looking for is, how can I get out of pain? How can I eat the foods I love again? How can I have the smile I've always wanted? How can I look good at my son's impending wedding? How can I look good at my 20-year reunion, or how can I look good now that I've entered the dating scene?

They are not there looking for the things that most dentists think that they are looking for. They are there looking for purely selfish, solve-my-problem reasons.

Colin: If they've got a problem in their mouth, why aren't they looking for a dentist?

Matt: Well, they're not looking for a dentist. They just want a way to make whatever that problem is go away. It doesn't necessarily have to be, I want the dentist closest to my neighborhood, or I want the dentist that I went to as a kid. Maybe they've not gone to a dentist in a while and they need to find somebody who is the expert in solving their problem.

Colin: When you say "their problem," you mean that very selfishly, like you said. It's their pain, their dentures. They're wanting a permanent solution to bite into that apple, if you're a patient that maybe has dentures.

Let's role-play here. Say I'm a patient that's had dentures for 20 years. I have no teeth left in my mouth and I'm tired of taking my teeth out every night and putting them in the cup next to the bed. What might I search for online?

Matt: If I'm a person who uses dentures and I'm tired of using dentures, I might search for "how can I get rid of my dentures." "My dentures hurt; what can I do about that?" "Is there a better solution than dentures?" They're not asking the things that a lot of dentists would think they would ask because dentists think like dentists. Dentists think about it in their terms. They're experts and they think about it the way they would think about it. You've got to think about how that normal, average, everyday person is going to ask that question, and then you want to have your content focus on answering those questions.

Colin: When you're writing good content, it sounds to me like you're really trying to satisfy two different parts. You're trying to satisfy the needs of the person searching and answering their questions and problems, but you're also trying to optimize that content for Google to get Google to rank your site highly. How do you balance those against each other?

Matt: That's a really, really good observation. In the past, focusing on Google was really the way most marketing companies went about creating their content. It was like making a chocolate chip cookie. A chocolate chip cookie is nothing but a chip delivery system, and it just can't be that way anymore.

Colin: When you say "a chip delivery system," you're essentially saying that the chocolate chips are like the keywords, that you sprinkle in your keywords and then you give out the chocolate chips, versus now what's different?

Matt: Right now, Google has gotten really smart about doing what we in marketing and lots of marketing companies used to do. That was to put in a lot of keywords. That way, it would make, it seemed to Google, like that page or your site was really authoritative on that particular issue.

Well, Google has gotten a lot smarter, and Google makes changes every year, not just a big change but changes over and over again. It's making changes so now Google is smart enough to see when you've only dropped in a few keywords but the rest of your content's not good.

Now, you can't just drop in keywords like "chocolate chips." You have to deliver the whole candy bar. That means that all of your content has to be good, whether that's your videos, whether that's your onsite content, whether that's graphics that you use, or white papers. Google is looking for things that are indicators, more like time on page. How many times did somebody share that content? It's not enough just to have good keywords. You do want to have that, but now, instead of being the indicator, it's just an indicator.

Colin: Google made somewhere around 600 changes to their algorithm last year. How do you keep up with that?

Matt: Well, it's awfully hard because much like Kentucky, where I'm from, KFC doesn't give away its secret herbs and spices. You have to watch what's going on in search engine results. There are lots of people who professionally watch what goes on.

We have people, of course, here at SmartBox who watch changes that Google makes, and then you have to be able to respond to that. It's a full-time job to figure out what works on Google and what changes you need to make.

I know we have a lot of dentists who are watching today that want to DIY their marketing, but the content part is an overwhelming thing. We have a whole department here that's devoted to creating great content for our clients so they can focus on what they really do best, which is dentistry.

Colin: What kind of content? You're a dentist and you're doing content marketing. What is content marketing? What are you creating? Are you just posting blogs on a website? What are you doing to create this content?

Matt: There are lots of different kinds of content. We can start with the most visible part of a dentist's marketing, which is their website. Well, those pages don't just come into creation out of the blue. Somebody has to write that content. Unfortunately, there are companies out there that want to use the same content over and over again for multiple websites.

Colin: Like duplicating it? Cloning it? Templating the content on the site?

Matt: Exactly.

Colin: I didn't know people still did that.

Matt: Yeah, we have seen instances where we've had people come on as a client and I can remember this; it happened to me specifically that I went to look at two different clients, one in the northeast and one down in Texas. I was reviewing their old website, looking for the kind of things they do, what sort of content we were going to need to write, and I couldn't believe it. They had the exact same content on their websites, one in the northeast and one in Texas. It was the exact same content.

Colin: When you find something like that, how does Google treat that? Why don't you want duplicate content?

Matt: That's not only bad in terms of it may not be specifically related to your practice, but from Google's standpoint, that's a big no-no. Google looks at that and not only says, "Oh, we've seen this content before, so we're not going to rate it very highly," but Google looks at that and says, "We've seen this content before. We're going to push you down the search engine results because we know this is duplicate content."

Colin: If you were going to put it on a bumper sticker: "Don't use duplicate content." Is that fair?

Matt: Absolutely, because Google is looking for content that is unique and fresh and a value to people. If you've got that content all over multiple websites, then it's going to make Google logically ask, "How valuable is this content?"

Colin: We should make some bumper stickers up for docs and sell them. I think that might be a good alternative market if dental marketing doesn't take off.

Matt: Yeah. We talked about your website content. That's one that's the most obvious part of your content, but then there are other parts of content, certainly, that we have found to be effective, for instance, like blogs. We write blogs for all of our clients. Sometimes almost every day, we're putting out a blog for a client on our highest packages. That is to show Google, "Hey, we're really knowledgeable in this area."

More important than showing Google that we're knowledgeable in this area and that we keep our website updated, it shows prospects that our dentists are the experts, that our dentists know the problems they have, our dentists can solve their problems. It lets us write for our dentists in a way that lets prospects know our dentist's personality, lets them know who our dentist is, the things that are important to them so that that content means something to the person who is looking for whatever they've searched.

Colin: Not only are you balancing against trying to have great optimized content and talking to the person, but you're also trying to set yourself up as the expert?

Matt: Right.

Colin: They're dentists. Why do they want to be the expert?

Matt: Of course, as all dentists know, there is competition. U.S. News & World Report just listed dentistry as the most desirable profession in the United States. It projected a 15 percent increase in new dentists over the next, I think it was 15 years. If you think competition is tight now in the dental field, it's about to get a lot tighter over the next few years. We really want to help dentists distinguish themselves, not as an expert, which most people expect their dentist to be, but the expert in their market.

Colin: A few other stats that I remember coming from that article were not only the number of dentists that are increasing but average spending from the United States consumer since 2008 has not increased at all, not increased at all. Not only do you have more dentists, you have flat spending from the consumer public and then let's not miss the big pink elephant in the room: corporate dentistry. More dentists are going into corporate dentistry than ever before. Corporate dentistry's marketing budget is humongous. They have the economies of scale and they have the marketing dollars to literally drive the private fee-for-service dentist out of business.

Tell me a little bit more. How do you differentiate yourself? How does a private fee-for-service dentist position himself against the corporate overlords in terms of content marketing and their perception in the market?

Matt: Content is actually one of the best ways to do that because when you're doing your onsite content, when you are writing your blogs – and we haven't even talked about video or graphics or some of the other visual things you can do on your website – but those are things that you can do that really relate to only you.

These corporate dentists are most likely going to use these template sites. Most of their pages are going to be the same as they would in Louisville, Kentucky, or Denver, Colorado, or wherever. They're going to have the exact same cookie-cutter look, the exact same cookie-cutter content.

Our dentists at SmartBox, we write all of their content. We create all of their videos. We do all of their visuals. Everything we do from a content standpoint is specifically about that dentist. That's how we really separate them from every other dentist, corporate or otherwise, in their marketplace.

Colin: We've got hundreds of dentists that we work with. How are you creating all this individualized content for all these doctors?

Matt: Well, it takes a lot of time. It takes a lot of manpower. We have some really, really fantastic folks in our production departments, whether that's in our writing department or whether that's in our video department. We really go out and look for the best and brightest. We've very serious about handpicking only the right people to come in, and then we give them good training about what it takes to attract more and better patients for our clients.

Colin: Awesome. We talked a little bit about onsite content. We talked about blogs briefly. What other kinds of content are there that dentists need to be doing to leverage the whole umbrella of what content is?

Matt: Video is a really good one. There are all kinds of statistics that show how video on the web continues to grow every year. Any dentist that is not using video is not missing the wave of the future. They're missing the wave of the present. Video is a must-have. It says what words take pages and pages to say – you could say in a really short video. Forrester marketing has said that one minute of video is worth 1.8 million words. That's pretty strong.

It's a really good way not only to talk about the things that your prospects are looking for but also to give an idea of your personality, to give an idea of who you are. There's no get-to-know-you period in dentistry anymore. There's no come in and get to meet me and see if I'm the dentist that you might like to have. People want to know that before they ever set that appointment. Video is really the best way to do that.

Colin: Awesome, awesome. What other things haven't we talked about here that are important if you're a dentist looking to put together a content marketing campaign? What kind of strategies or what other tips would you give to that dentist?

Matt: I'll tell you the one thing that we've not talked about that becomes increasingly important, and that's social media. I know in the past, we have been less than really eager to push our dentists into social media, and we still don't feel like it's a good use of our client's time or their staff resources to have somebody whose only job is to sit and tweet or Facebook post or whatever.

Social media you like to use all day long. There's just not a good ROI on that, but there are some really smart things dentists can do. There are things we do for our clients and that is to use your content in multiple channels. You might have a blog post on your website and then you might also post that to Facebook or also post that to LinkedIn so that you're really doubling the effectiveness of that piece of content.

Google is looking really strongly at social shares, at time on page, things that show there's engagement. The more channels you can put that content through, the more engagement you can get.

Colin: Matt, what advice would you give to the dentist that maybe has an old website that's maybe template or cookie-cutter? They know they have duplicate content. They know they've never written any great content for their website, or maybe you're talking to a dentist that's trying to DIY, do it yourself. What kind of advice would you give to that group?

Matt: The first and probably biggest piece of advice I would give is make sure that your content emphasizes that prospects can trust you, because trust is really the basis of what anybody wants in their dentist. They trust that you're going to solve their problems. They trust that you're going to do it in the least painful way possible. They trust that you're going to do it the least expensive way for them possible. Most importantly, they trust that you're going to do it the best way possible, that you are there looking out for them.

All of your content, whether that's onsite web content, whether that's blogs, whether that's videos, whether that's webinars like this one, whether it's white papers, whether it's podcasts, whatever it is, make sure that when you're done, you feel like the prospect who sees it knows that they can trust you.

The important thing with content just generally is to make sure that the content is what matters, that what you are saying – the message – comes across. If you handle the message, then the SEO, the search engine optimization, will take care of itself, not the other way around. Don't start off with, "How am I going to shoehorn these key ideas or these key search terms?" or, "Somebody went into my Google analytics and told me the five most common ways people find me are these search terms, so what can I write around that to get people on there?" It just doesn't work that way anymore.

I would definitely encourage dentists to do that. For dentists who can accomplish that, who can create great content, then they're in a much better position to combat corporate dentistry. They're in a much better position to go fee-for-service. They're in a much better position to bring in large-case dentistry.

For all those dentists out there who wish, "I wish didn't have to do all this drill-and-fill dentistry," or, "I wish I could only focus on these niches" – focus content on those niches, bring in the kind of patients that you want via that content, and you'll really succeed.

Content is one of your highest ROI, return on investment, measures that you can actively track and follow. You can see which pages are people going to, which things resonate with patients, which of my calls to action on my pages get the most traction and therefore which content seems to make the biggest difference. Content is really the basis around which you run your marketing.

Colin: For those dentists that want to get an evaluation of their content marketing, whether it be limited just to "Hey, is this content working for me? Is it generating new patients and phone calls into my practice?" or look at a more extensive Patient Attraction System, give one of our new practice consultants a call, who will be glad to share what we can do with you and more importantly, a strategy that can take you to where you want to go, complimentary on us.

I appreciate you being on the show, Matt.

Matt: Yeah, thanks for having me.

Colin: Thanks for chatting about content. It's been awesome to learn about the new developments and what dentists need to be doing to succeed and attract the patients that they want in this 2016 and beyond Google era.

Thanks for joining us for another Inside Patient Attraction™. I hope this month is a fantastic month for you. I appreciate your time, taking time out of your busy day, out of your busy practice, your busy lives, your family to join us for 20 or 30 minutes to look at how you can improve your practice and what it takes in 2016, 2017, and beyond to be competitive if you're a private fee-for-service dentist.

Thank you again for your time. I look forward to talking to you again on another episode.

Dental Content Marketing

Matt Tungate appeared again on the December 2016 episode of

the Inside Patient Attraction™ series to discuss how dentists can use content marketing to follow up with new prospects until they're ready to choose a dentist to perform the dental procedures they want or need.

Inside Patient Attraction™ December 2016

Colin: If you're a dentist looking for more and better patients, dominating Google is one thing that you know you've got to do to make that happen, but once you've got them to your website, what are you going to do with them? How are you going to get them to know you, and like you, and trust you, and ultimately call your practice in a point?

That's exactly what we're going to talk about on this December episode of Inside Patient Attraction™. Thanks for joining us today. I'm Colin Receveur, and today I want to talk about on-demand dental marketing. We're joined today by our Director of Content here at SmartBox, Matt.

Matt, thanks for being on the show.

Matt: Hey, Colin. Thanks, man. I always love to be on.

Colin: We're going to talk today about what you can do to convert more and better patients into your practice. How are you going to get these patients to know you, and like you, and trust you after you've already got them to your website? What are these pieces of content and marketing that you've got to have? We've laid out several of them that we want to talk about today, from email marketing systems, to press releases, to books and ghostwritten material, to blogs, and articles – all these different kinds of things that we want to talk about, the approach and where you use these different kinds of pieces, because frankly, there's a lot of misinformation out there. There's a lot of internet marketing companies that want to use these in different ways that aren't really how they're intended and for no benefit of the dentist. We're going to lay it all out today on this episode and talk about ...

Let's start with email marketing campaigns. That's probably the one that most dentists are most used to hearing about. Everybody's heard of email marketing campaigns. What are dentists doing, and how are they leveraging email marketing to attract more and better patients, Matt?

Matt: Right. I think really the most effective way to use email marketing is automated email marketing. I know when we use our Patient Attraction System™, it's a big part of what we do. If a dentist can not only attract a prospect to his or her website but then stay in touch with that prospect, they are much more likely to convert that prospect into a patient. Ultimately, that is the goal of any dentist's web marketing.

With an automated email campaign the prospect comes to the website, and they give information to the dentist. Of course with our clients, we give them top-notch lures that attract that prospect's attention, offer them something that makes them want to give their information, name, and email address usually. Then after that, they will receive a string of emails, usually over the span of four or five months, to help them understand why that dentist not only is a good option for solving their dental problem but the best option for solving their dental problem.

Colin: Why are we trying to continue to communicate to these patients over four or five months? What's the advantage there?

Matt: Sure. The advantage there is patients very rarely, for high-end dentistry – your implants, your dentures, your ortho – are very unlikely at that first opportunity to say, "Yeah. Go ahead and sign me up for that." You know, you're talking about somebody that's going to drop 15 or 25 thousand dollars. They're going to need to think about that for a minute usually, so while they are deciding not only, "Do I want to go forward with this procedure?" but, "With whom?" you are the dentist, if you're emailing them saying, "Hey. Thanks for coming in. Please be thinking about the benefits of that implant," and then the next week they might get an email that says, "Hey. Been thinking about you. Really want to make sure that you understand that you're likely to live 10 years longer if you have a dental implant," and you do that week after week after week, you stay in front of that prospect, so that when they make the decision, "Yes, I need a dental implant," they have an obvious choice, and that's the person that's been staying in contact with them over all that time.

Colin: There was a cool study done last year by Google, you may be aware of it, that ... they've called it their ZMOT Study, where they said that people reference 10.4 sources of information before they make that buying decision. I think that sounds like exactly what you're talking about here. People want to get all this information and be courted, so to speak, before they're going to see you as the expert and choose you to be the guy that's going to do the work.

Matt: Right. Absolutely. The best part about doing this automatically is the dentist never has to touch it. With our clients, for instance, we write those sequences of emails for our clients right up front. They make sure they're happy with all of the content, and then we set that out to go, as I like to say it, to go out "automagically," so that the dentist never has to touch that at all. It just happens behind the scenes so that that dentist and his staff can focus on what they're really there to do, which is to run that practice.

Colin: Very cool, very cool. How are you sending it out? What are you using to do that automagically?

Matt: We've had a lot of success with a program called Infusionsoft®. It's one of the ways that we send out that automated email marketing campaign. It's really consistent. It gives us really good results, and we get a lot of really good information on the prospects that open those emails.

Colin: Awesome, awesome. What kind of results are you seeing from using these direct marketing systems?

Matt: We find that dentists get few tire kickers and they get more patients who come in asking, "When can we set this up?" not, "What is this you're wanting me to do?" because that email marketing campaign helps inform them. It helps separate out the people who are serious about having it done from the people who aren't, and one of the side benefits of it is it keeps people from wasting the dentist's time.

Colin: The prospects are more educated when they come into the practice.

Matt: Right. By the time they come back, they know why they want to have it done. Their only question is, "When can you fit me in?"

Colin: The email marketing campaign is the piece that is the drip behind, it's the constant flow up that builds that trust and rapport. How do you get people's email addresses? What are you doing to get their attention? How do you get their buy-in, if you want to call it that?

Matt: Sure. For our marketing clients, we offer a dental lure, as we call it, and it is some great, little, visible, visual thing on the client's website that says something really intriguing, something like, "Don't die with your teeth in a glass," or, "Let us tell you how a better smile can change your life," something that's going to grab that prospect's attention and they're going to say, "Oh. I'd like to know more about that." It's generally something that we have identified with our doctor that's a pointed emphasis for their marketing. If they want to emphasize implants, we might go with something like, "Don't die with your teeth in a glass." If it's veneers or whatever, it'd be something more targeted toward that.

When the prospect comes, clicks that they're interested in that, we say, "Hey, listen. If you'll give us this little bit of information …" Again, we usually use name and email address. They're low barriers of entry, meaning that people are pretty much okay with giving you that standard information. It doesn't stop them from proceeding. Once they give us that information, we generally offer them something like, "Hey. Let us send you this free report all about implants," or ortho, or whatever the topic at hand is. That's what starts the sequence. That's their okay that it's okay for the dentist to send them future emails, and so immediately they get that really nice, long informational report, and then the follow-up sequence begins after that.

Colin: What about other types of written materials? What else are you finding very effective for these large elective-case dentists who give out to their patients to build their expertise and their expert status?

Matt: Yeah. That is an excellent question. Books are another thing that we have found, especially for our high-end clients, really, really work well. If a dentist is really looking for better patients, as opposed to just more patients, we find that a book is really effective.

Colin: Why a book?

Matt: Well, I mean, the saying "He wrote the book on it" is a saying for a reason. Colin: It's pretty powerful if you have written the book.

Colin: It's pretty powerful if you have written the book.

Matt: Right. One of the things that sometimes clients will be concerned about is, "I don't have time to write a book," and some of the people watching this episode may understand that, if you can imagine what it takes to write a book. What we do for our dentist is we ghostwrite that book for them. It has their name on it. They give plenty of input and direction on that book, but we take our talented team of writers and they compile that information. They put it together. That way, we know it's technically sound. We know that it's at a readability level that most people can understand, and we know that it will be effective in getting that prospect from the information-gathering stage to the decision-making stage.

Colin: Why doesn't everybody write a book? Every dentist could write their own book if they had the time. What's your thoughts on that?

Matt: Well, time is certainly the biggest issue. If you've got time to write a book, then you need our help. We need to get you some more patients in. Besides the time, some dentists we have seen have tried writing books, and they have a hard time writing for prospects. They want to write for other dentists. They're so concerned that they have to call a prophy a prophy and that they have to use a lot of dental terminology that it just goes over their prospect's head. That doesn't convert.

One of the things that we try to do is we take dentalese and we convert that into generally a junior high reading level, because we want people who have low literacy to still be able to understand what's going on. I want to make sure that dentists understand, especially the younger dentists out there, we work with a lot of really, really experienced, tenured dentists, and a misconception is that blue-collar people may not have money for elective dentistry.

I know of a great story where there was a factory worker who retired, and he had saved his whole work life to replace the missing teeth that he had lost in his youth. He goes and sees that dentist – and that dentist may be watching this, so he'll know that I'm telling the story – he goes and he basically lays out a briefcase of $25,000 and says, "I want you to take care of this. It's always been an embarrassment for me. Now that I'm retired, this is what I want. This is what I want to do with my retirement. I want to finally be happy with how I look."

Dentists should not assume that they are only marketing to a certain demographic of people. That's why we write at that reading level. That money is there. Those people that you may think not have the means to do that may have the means to do that, and of course people with higher education, more affluence, they read right through that, and they get the information they need.

Colin: Something I've seen a lot with the demographics of patients that go after those large cases is that the patients that are in what we'll call the white-collar class grew up in the white-collar class, and they had the access to dental care, so they don't have the problems that the blue-collar class has. They had access to great dental care, and dentistry, and good practices. You see a lot more blue-collar people, demographics, that need that large, elective, restorative dentistry. So many people draw out of their 401(k)s to pay for these procedures. Make sure you're not going after too affluent of a group, because there's a huge, huge opportunity in that blue-collar area, socioeconomically, that need and can pay for these large procedures.

Matt: That may be a good topic for a future webisode.

Colin: That may be a good topic. We'll have to mark that down. We'll have to write that down. You write these books. You write the reports. You've got the email. This is all the expertise-building information. What do you do with it after you write it?

Matt: The book specifically, the way we encourage our patients to do that is to use those books for the patients that are at that information state. Somebody's come in. They've had the exam. You've given them the information. They seem on the fence. That's a great follow-up. You can either have them out the door or you print them on-demand. There's another touch point. You follow up with them saying, "Hey. We know you're trying to make this decision. Please have this complimentary book that explains more about the procedure." It's a fantastic follow-up. It gives them information to make a decision. Again, you're the guy who wrote the book when they decide they want to have that procedure done.

Colin: Awesome, awesome. What other kinds of content are you producing to help dentists set themselves apart?

Matt: Another good long-form, like a book but not as formal as a book, is a white paper. White papers are really, really excellent for if you have a specific expertise. We have quite a few of our dentists who are leading in the field of one aspect of dentistry or another. If you've done independent research, or you've developed a new technique, or you've developed a new tool, as some of our dentists have, those are fantastic white papers to write about: "This is how this benefits patients, and we just happen to have a hand in that."

Even if not, even if you're like your dad, who has so many hours of training and has even gone overseas for training with some of the elite dentists in the world, he would be a prime candidate, another dentist, to write a white paper about the effects of implants on your life, that just go beyond short reading, but they're not printed like a book. A white paper – the way we do it for our clients is you would have a white paper and it would be on your site, downloadable or could be delivered by email, so that, again, it establishes that expertise, but it's more readily available. The problem they say with instant gratification is it just doesn't happen fast enough. That's a way to get that person who's very hot right then the information they need.

Colin: Matt, at the beginning of this I promised our viewers that I was going to tell them what not to do, what to look out for. Let's talk a little bit about changes in the content world. What things have we found that don't really generate a great ROI that doctors should pay close attention to if they're doing?

Matt: Yeah. There are a couple of traditional things that we find that a lot of clients are doing when they come on board with us that we've just never found to deliver a good enough ROI to offer. The first would be newsletters. I know dentists, especially dentists who've been practicing a long time, they love newsletters. At one time, that was a very cutting-edge, creative thing to do it on paper. Right? You could send out a newsletter to all your patients. Man, people loved that. Then, oh lord, here came the internet, and you could suddenly put your ...

Colin: Your PDF.

Matt: Yeah. Yeah. You could email your PDF newsletter to everybody, and everybody had Microsoft Word, and boy, there were all these pretty templates that you could make these great newsletters. People just thought that was great. The problem is they've just become passe, and in fact, now they look dated. There are much better ways to do that same thing. In fact, you could argue that Facebook is really the e-newsletter of the 21st century. That's what we have found is a much better way to get that same kind of ongoing, updatey, personal type information that was always in the traditional e-newsletter. Social media is a much better way.

Colin: Much more currently.

Matt: Certainly. We certainly don't encourage our dentists to go and spend all day tweeting or Facebooking either, but that's just the more contemporary way of getting out that same information. Another thing that dentists – and even we, up until we got some data, you know, early this year that indicated to us that it just wasn't that effective – was press releases. We were very high on press releases when press releases were effective. As we and others in the industry noticed that press releases were losing their effectiveness, we have de-emphasized them too.

Press releases used to be a really great opportunity to generate search engine optimization, because Google would see those and say, "Hey. These people are movers and shakers. They've got authority." Google de-emphasized press releases in its search, and so now we really only want to spend our doctors' time and encourage them to only spend their time using press releases when there's really something that's going to be shareable or it's going to actually get press attention or going to get community involvement. Those things still make press releases, but I remember once upon a time we would tell dentists, "Listen. If you get a new piece of office furniture, let's go ahead and write a press release about it.

Colin: Do a press release. Yeah. Not anymore.

Matt: Right. Those days are just gone. It's not effective, and so we encourage obviously our clients, and to anybody who's watching this episode, don't let your PR company tell you that you're getting such a great deal because they do you two press releases a month. I mean, it's a fantastic ego stroke, but that's really about what it is.

Colin: Matt, there's all kinds of content that we haven't talked about here. How does that fit into the content puzzle?

Matt: Right. Absolutely. Hopefully we've got some viewers who saw earlier this year our Inside Patient Attraction episode on content. We talked a lot about blogs, and page content, FAQs, and things like that. Those things are still very relevant.

We, within the content department, we recently have diversified the types of content we've added to our toolbox, if you will, because we are finding that some of the old metrics that used to be important

– blogs had to be a certain length, and you had to have a certain number a month – Google, again, continues to change its algorithm, and we are finding that these things that our viewers have probably heard of, memes, and, like I said, FAQs, and little snippets, and Facebooks, and tweets, those things are all playing more into the algorithm, because Google sees that people use them and says, "Oh. That must be good content."

Colin: Must be.

Matt: Well, and maybe it is. Those are some of the things that we're talking about doing. I was just talking with one of our content experts today, and we had this idea for a funny meme. I'll go ahead and give it to you. I'll go ahead and give it to viewers for free right now. There's a famous scene out of one of *The Lord of the Rings* movies where one of the characters says, "One does not simply walk into Mordor," and it's become an internet huge meme.

Colin: Mm-hmm. Oh yeah. I've seen it.

Matt: We were talking one that would be hilarious in this current area that said, "One does not simply stop flossing." We just thought that dentists that use that, it's just a cute thing that could be shared, and it would show your personality a little bit.

Colin: It'd probably go viral.

Matt: It may. It very well may. The original idea we had was that it was originally going to be, "Dentists simply do not meme," and we just thought, "That's just not true. That's a passe idea." You know, those things are becoming more and more important to get shared, and get likes, and get your name out, and again, still trying to give a little bit of your personality and show who you are.

Colin: It's the new community involvement.

Matt: It absolutely is.

Colin: I'm going to get on my soapbox for a second here, Matt, because I see so many older dentists that, you know, their numbers are down. Their new patient numbers are down. Their practices are down. Their profits are down. You go to them, and you talk to them, and you say, "Well, what's changed?" The dentist goes, "Well, nothing's changed. I'm still doing it exactly like I did 20 years ago."

You say, "Well, how many community involvement things did you do 20 years ago? How many profit raisers or fundraisers I mean? How many Dentistry From The Heart things did you do 20 years ago?" The dentist goes, "Well, I was really involved in my community." You say, "How many have you done in the past 12 months?" "Well, none," you know, the grumpy old man. Right? That's exactly what we're talking about here. If you want people to recognize your name, your brand, and come to you, you've got to get your name in front of them.

Matt: Right. You've got to use the current techniques. That's the thing is, I've heard you say numerous times it used to be, once upon a golden age of dentistry, you just hung your shingle out and everybody came to you. Then you put out a Yellow Pages ad and everybody came to you. Well, you could do both of those things today. It's just not going to get you very far. You've got to go along with the times.

Colin: Yup. Follow the times. Viewers of this Inside Patient Attraction know that I've said, "Dentistry's a decade behind medicine." If you want to see what's coming, look where medicine is today. That's where dentistry will be in 10 years. If you don't keep evolving, like Jack Trout said, famously, "Evolve or die."

Matt: Yeah. Well, I would argue that for the viewers of this web episode, they're already ahead of the curve.

Colin: Absolutely.

Matt: While their competitors are sitting at home right now …

Colin: Playing golf, maybe.

Matt: Maybe…. they're obviously trying to keep themselves up-to-date and doing it in a very current way by watching a web episode, so kudos to you, and congratulations on being on the leading edge of the curve. Hopefully some of the things we just talked about will keep you there.

Colin: Well, awesome to have you on the show, Matt.

Matt: Sure, man.

Colin: I appreciate you coming here and sharing some of the awesome things that we're doing with on-demand marketing, with content marketing, that can help dentists who attract the patients that they want, more and better patients, and ultimately more freedom, because you build this thriving practice. You grow it to point that you don't have to work those long hours, nights, and weekends to live the life that you want to live, to have what you deserve. Thanks for being here, Matt. As always, keep moving forward.

And One for the Do-It-Yourselfers

Unless you're really into and very skilled at writing, you really don't want to spend countless hours producing your own dental content. It's something that the vast majority of dentists aren't good at.

But just in case you're itching to write your own content, here are some tips to help you do it more easily. This SmartBox blog posted in September 2016.

Where Do You Come Up with Your Dental Content Ideas?

If you're doing dental content marketing, and you should be, you already know that it can be tough to keep coming up with new ideas. New content is what allows you to stay in front of your dental prospect, establish a virtual relationship, and ultimately influence him or her to choose you to solve their dental problems.

Dentistry is not a very fast-moving profession. Compared to many other areas of society and business today, it's positively glacial. Dentists don't get to latch onto social crazes like Pokémon GO, the latest smartphone, Chia Pets (remember them?), or even the Macarena (better forgotten).

In an industry that rarely has "groundbreaking news," how do you find new and interesting topics to write about? You turn to the internet.

Back in June, Cision published a good guide to services that will alert you to trending topics. But unless you have the creativity to work dentistry into almost everything, that may not help you come up with ideas for your content writing.

Fortunately, you're not the only one writing content that's suitable for dental patients. You can get ideas from articles in trade journals, from the ADA website, and even from other dentists. Now, no one is suggesting that you use their content. But ideas are fair game, and if you can put your own unique, interesting spin on an idea, by all means, do.

A couple of caveats: When you're building off others' ideas, you'll do well to run your own writing through a plagiarism checker. You can invest in a paid app, or you can use one of the free online services. It's all too easy to unconsciously borrow someone's phrasing while you're writing about their idea.

There are companies out there offering paid dental content. In general, I'm not a fan of these services for one reason: that content won't be unique to your website. Google favors content that is unique, fresh, helpful, and authoritative. And Google has a really long memory. Since you're unlikely to be the first purchaser of packaged online content, you won't get the SEO credit for it. In fact, your website or blog is likely to be penalized in search rankings.

You can also get content ideas from your interactions with patients. For instance, by some estimates, over 140 million people in this country have some degree of dental fear or anxiety. If you came up with a novel idea to help someone deal with dental anxiety, that's something your prospects will definitely want to read about.

Patient success stories are always a good read. If you intervened early and decisively in a patient's periodontal disease, tell people about it. If you have the patient's permission to use their name, and a glowing testimonial, your writing will find an eager audience.

Lastly, not all your content writing has to be, or should be, about dentistry. Your prospects want to get to know the person behind the dental mask. You can write about everyday events outside the practice, goings-on with your staff, or last Sunday's sermon in church.

Your content writing should inform, educate, and entertain. Above all, it should subtly influence your reader to see you as the trusted dental expert to solve their problems. Ultimately, you want them to pick up the phone or make an appointment through your website.

The goal of content marketing is to get more and better patients. You'll achieve that by using your online content to build trust and credibility.

Websites and Website Development

Great dental content is a must for attracting more and better patients, but only if your website loads quickly and correctly across all devices. Otherwise, today's impatient dental prospects will click away and find another dentist.

If you had a marketing company do your dental website, how do you know you actually got what you need to attract more and better patients?

Tim Horst, SmartBox's Web Development Manager, joined me in January 2017 on our Inside Patient Attraction™ web series to discuss the must-haves for dental websites that will entice dental prospects to stay rather than click away.

Inside Patient Attraction™ January 2017

Colin: Welcome to Inside Patient Attraction™. I'm Colin Receveur and today, I'm going to be joined by Tim Horst, our Web Development Manager here SmartBox. Now, Tim, he leads up the team of web developers that we have that do all the backend coding for all of our dentists' sites. We'll be showing you by the end of today's episode things that you need to know so you're not sold a bill of goods and what you need to know, what's important to a dentist to know, about how this fits into the whole picture of the Patient Attraction System™ so that at the end of the day, you're getting more and better patients from your marketing.

Stick around.

Welcome back to Inside Patient Attraction. I'm here today with Tim Horst, our Web Development Manager, and we're going to be talking today about all the hype about web development standards and Google and how you are probably being oversold from other companies on what kind of development and SEO and backend structure you need to really attract more and better patients into your practice. Welcome here, Tim.

Tim: Thank you, Colin.

Colin: Honored to have you here and chat a little bit about what's going on in the web development world.

Tim: Thank you very much.

Colin: What you see day in and day out in your world? Tell me a little bit about what you spend your days doing.

Tim: Well, my day is spent ensuring that the development for all of our doctors' websites is taken care of in a timely fashion, well built, maintained, and structured in such that our sites load and perform as best they can.

Colin: Awesome. How has that evolved over the years? Hell, you've been doing this for 20 years.

Tim: Twenty years, yeah.

Colin: How have you seen things change over the last 20 years?

Tim: Well, it's changed tremendously. Twenty years ago, we spent our time full-blown, all day writing code. Every code was developed and written specifically for the site that was being launched at the time. It was all static. There was no dynamic, real dynamic, capabilities. If you wanted something to interact with a database or such, you'd have to write 25, 35, 40 lines of code just for that interaction alone.

Colin: Whereas today, we have technologies like WordPress for instance, that it's all built in and it just happens.

Tim: All built in. It does all the heavy lifting for you – if you want it out of the box, it's there to do what you need it to do. But that being said, our developers customize and build functionalities specifically for our doctors' needs.

Colin: Tell me about your development team.

Tim: Well, we have nine developers on staff. Their responsibilities include theme development, site builds, look-and-feel and such. As I mentioned before, we do plugin development, unique items that a doctor's site will need to interact. We have a line manager whose responsibility is ensuring that all the tasks and all the builds are kept on time, and we also have a full-time QA analyst.

Colin: What's the QA do?

Tim: A QA ensures that the build, the content, imagery, everything on the site is as it should be for the launch.

Colin: Quality assurance.

Tim: Quality assurance.

Colin: How does the way that we do it here at SmartBox, with custom building these for each doctor with developing specific needs, how does that differ from other places out there like I've heard of from Wix, or these template cookie-cutter websites? Tell me a little bit about the differences.

Tim: That's exactly it. They're cookie-cutter. There's no customization. You're very limited in to what you can choose for a look-and-feel aspect of a website. You are limited also in the functionalities that you can achieve with your website.

There's no ability to have any specific unique need that you would need for your site to be built; you have to rely on the only things that they offer to get what you're looking for.

Colin: How do the sites that SmartBox builds differ from ... We've heard of Wix and these sites that, boom, 30 minutes later, they pop up and they're there for the doctor. How does what we do differ in terms of what we do and the results that it gets and why for our doctors versus using those other cookie-cutter type alternatives?

Tim: Well, they're cookie-cutter, you're going to get the same thing that everybody else that's using that service is going to get: a non-unique website, a website that performs at the same level that their other clients or customers perform at. We have the ability to customize the site. We have the ability to take things like page speed, site optimization, image optimization, load times, these factors in and then customize the website so that we can optimize the speeds to make it perform as well as possible for the doctor.

Colin: What's that mean for the doctor?

Tim: Oh, the doctor is going to get better page rankings in SEO. They're going to get a better user experience, because the user is not going to be frustrated because the site's not loading or that it's missing images, or they're not able to interact with it and it's going to ultimately give them back an ROI that is going to be positive for them.

Colin: I've often told doctors that cheap marketing and cheap websites are the most expensive, because it's a complete flush down the toilet.

Tim: It is, it is. Again, because you're getting the same thing that everybody else gets for that set price. The minute you start needing new functionality or if you want to incorporate some third-party software, if you want to track, or if you want to interact with some marketing campaigns, you're going to end up paying a lot more money for it if it has that ability to do it.

Colin: Speaking of load times, how does page speed, and how fast your website loads – why should a doctor care about that?

Tim: Well, the two main points of load time, page speed are related to SEO rankings. Google's algorithm highlights how fast a site loads as to how it's going to rank its site and user experience. You want your user to be able to interact with your website in order to get the information that they're going to need.

Colin: Nobody wants to wait on a site to load like they did in 1994?

Tim: Nobody wants to wait on the site to load, no.

Colin: How fast are some of our newest sites loading right now?

Tim: There was a study done a number of years ago that decided that the optimum time for a page to load was two seconds.

Colin: That's pretty quick.

Tim: They figure anything after two seconds, that the user isn't going to stick around to interact with it, whether it's to buy something or to fill out a form, or anything like that, so we've been eyeing that two seconds as a top-end right now, but in actuality, most of our new client sites are coming in under one second.

Colin: That's smoking.

Tim: Yeah. We concentrate on a lot of points to achieve those things. We have tuned our servers to have them serve up the sites as fast as they can. We have optimized all the images that come in on a site to make them as small and as fast as possible. We leaned out the code as much we can. We take WordPress's core, we strip it down as much as we can. We eliminate all the extra calls that are on there. We implement Google's products such as tag manager to ensure that third-party scripts come in at the right time in a load sequence.

Colin: Sounds a lot like a race car. What about ... Mobile is a big topic these days. Tell me about the history of mobile and where are we today with mobile friendliness.

Tim: Well, mobile development over the last decade, or even longer than that, has changed dramatically in that time span and also in a year-to-year time span. Every year it seems to be evolving more and more. Twelve years ago, on very little screens all you would get, the little screens, you would get a few words of text here and there. Then the advent of smartphones came out and higher resolution, the ability to start actually interacting with websites fully on a phone, has really thrown the web development world in a whole other track.

It used to be that we built websites and then considered the mobile aspect of it afterwards. Now it's flipped. It's the other way around. You look at mobile devices as the mainstay of what you are building. Desktops and laptops, not a byproduct, but it's the everyday world of it, so we want to ensure that the sites perform on devices almost more than they perform on the laptops and the desktops. A decade ago, it started off that you would have what they call an adaptive site, and those were all pure static sites. There was no real interactivity or anything like that. It was just a static version of a stripped-down website of yours.

Colin: What if you have that in today's world still?

Tim: That would mean you'd lose clients. The ability to look at a website and interact with the telephone numbers or – everybody interacts with the maps on them now, the locations, how do I get to where I want to go with what I'm seeing right now – does not exist in an adaptive site. But in a responsive site, which is your current website, is served across all devices, whether it's a desktop, whether it's a tablet, whether it's a laptop, or whether it's a phone, it's the same website; it just responds to the device that you are on.

Colin: How many different kinds of devices can our websites today respond to?

Tim: Our sites respond to every device that's out on the market. We have looked at all of the Windows-based devices, the Android-based devices, the iOS devices, whether they're phones, whether they're tablets, laptops, or desktops to ensure that the sites function and look as good as they can across all of them.

Colin: The goal is to have it look perfect no matter what size screen or what resolution or what magnification the client, the prospect, the patient, is actually searching for that dentist on.

Tim: Exactly. It looks the same across all of them, meaning an experience. Obviously, the elements change a little bit because the screens are smaller and stuff, but it's the experience we consider first.

Colin: How does a doctor that has a mobile website, how do they know if what they have is old or new, good or bad, in compliance with Google or not – how can they self-diagnose what they have?

Tim: It's all the time frame. Google in itself updates yearly with their algorithms, and if the site was built more than a year ago, you really need to look at it again because it's going to be outdated. It's not going to be performing as best as it can for the user. I mean, this is something we do all the time. We look at incoming clients, things that they had done in the past, how can we improve on them and how can we imply that to help them achieve more ROI.

Colin: Web development, a very technical cited subject, but a lot of information about what dentists need to be doing to attract more and better patients into their practice. It's all part of the Patient Attraction System™. You can have a great design, you can have your video, you can have the follow-up, you can even have the tracking, but if you don't have the backend, if you don't have the optimizable backend, the fast page speed, and if you're not staying up-to-date with these standards, whether it's the optimization or the mobile standards, you're not going to be found and you're going to fall behind.

Well, Tim, thanks for being on the show.

Tim: Thank you very much.

Colin: Appreciate your time hanging out a little bit, talking to our awesome dentists about what they can do to attract more patients, attract better patients, because that's the name of the game, so thanks for being on the show and as always, keep moving forward.

Dentists Must Go Mobile or Go Home

Mobile and mobile-compatible websites were all over the marketing news in 2016, and for good reason. Searches from mobile devices have overtaken searches from desktops and laptops and continue to pull away.

If your dental prospects are searching for a dentist on a mobile device, make sure they can not only find your website but can easily access and read everything you want to show them on those tiny screens.

Patient Attraction Episode 929

Google announced in late August of this year that web pages that don't meet its new, stricter mobile criteria will be downgraded in search results in 2017. That's only one reason why dentists need to go mobile. I'll be back after the break to tell you more. Stay tuned.

Thanks for watching the Patient Attraction Podcast™. I'm Colin Receveur.

Mobile search overtook desktop search in 2015, and the gap is continuing to widen. And it's not just search – a recent report indicated that 51 percent of digital content is viewed on mobile devices compared to 42 percent for desktops.

Most companies have taken note of the change in emphasizing mobile-friendly online content. In fact, Google noted that some 85 percent of pages are now mobile-friendly, where the text can be read without scrolling or zooming and links are easy to tap. So the mobile-friendly label will soon be a thing of the past, and Google is pushing new, stricter criteria.

One of the big things that Google will penalize are mobile popup ads beginning in January of 2017. Google believes that popups on a mobile screen disrupt the user's experience. Those popups can include opt-in/opt-out notifications, which many dentists use. Legally required popups, such as for age verification, are fine. Otherwise, some care in how you handle notifications is in order. If you have low-participation opt-in popups, you might consider getting rid of them.

As it always has, internet success means giving people what they want in the way they want it. Keep that in mind with your mobile pages and notifications, and you should do fine. HOWEVER: Your content has to be up to standard as well, because mobile compatibility isn't the only thing you can take a hit on.

Join me for our next podcast. Until tomorrow, keep moving forward.

Another Perspective: 15 Minutes with Dr. Howard Farran

I think wisdom is where you find it, and Howard has a lot of wisdom to share. I've certainly learned from him, and I hope he might have found one or two of my tips to be useful.

He's well on his way to being a legend in dental marketing circles. He's a practicing dentist with an MBA. He's also the owner of Farran Media, which includes Dentaltown.com, Orthotown.com, Hygienetown.com, TodaysDental.com, FarranMedia.com, and HowardFarran.com.

He joined me on the Patient Attraction Podcast™ to share his tips for what makes a dental practice successful.

Patient Attraction Podcast™ 397
15 Minutes With Dr. Howard Farran

Colin: Welcome to the Patient Attraction Podcast™. I've got Dr. Howard Farran here today. I appreciate you coming on the show today, thank you.

Howard: It's an honor.

Colin: Thank you. I hear you're doing some comedy club stuff in your spare time.

Howard: It's always been a hobby of mine. I've just always loved ... When I was in college, I used to do any open mic night. I think when I lecture, I get a lot of my comedy ya-yas out, but sometimes when I'm back home, I always like to hit the local clubs.

Colin: That's fun. We went down to a local club, wife and I – I've never been a lot into them – but we go down there occasionally and see who's on stage. It's always for a good night. It makes for a good time.

Howard: It's funny for me because when I do comedy clubs in

Phoenix, Scottsdale, Mesa, Tempe, all those cities, they always sit there and say, "Oh my God, you're the cleanest act. You don't say the f-word. You're just a 52-year-old grandpa. You're the cleanest act in town. All the other comedians are all vulgar." Then when I go into dentistry with that exact same mojo act, now I'm the wildest speaker in dentistry. It's all context. What you can say to a guy at church versus in a fishing boat are just two different mediums.

Colin: So you're still practicing?

Howard: I am. I think that when you don't have to do something, then you just do it for love. I don't have to do it. My four boys are raised. I've got a 3-year-old granddaughter. I got a dental magazine, a website. I like to lecture. Now I don't have to do anything, now it's 10 times more fun because I want to. Also, Dentaltown is the only media company that's actually owned by a real-live short, fat, bald dentist. I think that keeps it real. I won't talk about anything unless we use it in our office. When we use it in our office, we buy it with our own money. I think it's a really good ... keeping it real, keeping it fun.

A lot of stuff that flies across my desk, "You should do this, advertise this," I'll show it to my dental assistant who's been with me 28 years, Jan, she's rolling her eyes and I'm rolling her eyes. We don't want to help promote something that we don't think is good for –

Colin: Really grounded in the trenches, so to speak.

Howard: Absolutely.

Colin: Tell me a little bit about what you're doing in marketing, in your practice. What are you finding to be successful?

Howard: I think marketing is pretty interesting. What I like to focus the most on is organic growth. I think since women make nine out of 10 appointments – women, if you lose their trust, they're not going to like you. They're not going to love you. They're not going to come see you. They're not going to stay married to you. Trust is everything with women. When they come in off blind marketing, they don't know you yet. They don't trust you yet. If you get 100 new people that can't pick you out of a police lineup, maybe only 20 percent are going to buy something, but if they are referred by a friend or a loved one – my friend Megan tells me to go to you, I already trust you. Now I'm far more likely to buy. I like to focus on the organic stuff.

I tell dentists all the time. They don't answer half their incoming calls. There's 168 hours in a week. They're only open 32 hours a week. That's only 19 percent of 168. Half the calls come in before 8 o'clock or after 5 o'clock.

Colin: Or on the hour lunch break.

Howard: Yeah, or on the hour lunch break. These are mostly organic calls. These are mostly someone who came in your office five years ago: "My neighbor just told me to call you." I firmly believe that if you own a Chinese restaurant, or pizza delivery, or a dental office, if a Chinese delivery all the sudden gets twice as many phone calls, what will happen to its sales?

Colin: It'll explode.

Howard: It'll double. The dentist doesn't answer half his calls. I firmly believe if those dentists got a digital phone system so they knew every incoming call, what the phone number was, the name attached, and spread out their receptionist to cover more … Look at it as a funnel. You don't have to make fillings, root canals, and crowns 60, 70 hours a week.

As far as the funnel catching those incoming organic calls … When you take the front desk and you split out and you say, "Instead of two girls Monday through Thursday 8-5 and an hour for lunch 12-1, I'm going to have Susie come in at 6 and have her do lunch 11-12 and leave at 2:30. I'm going to have Amy come in at 9:30, do lunch 1-2, stay till six."

If I can widen that net and get more people … I see the front desk as sales and marketing. The dentist, they always have more staff helping the dentist make the hamburger, fry, and the coke than up front. When you're understaffed up front and you answer every phone call, "Can you please hold," then you don't know why –

Colin: Then they hang up.

Howard: Yeah, and then you don't know why you don't have any revenue.

Colin: We've always seen the phone call trends on a 24-hour day. Eleven to two is the hot area. That's when most of your calls – well, not most, but the highest volume by hour 11-2. So many offices I see, that's when they take their lunch. Nobody's there. I 100 percent agree with you on that. There's so much lost opportunity.

Howard: Firemen don't get to pick a lunch. Police officers don't get to pick a lunch. Emergency rooms don't get to pick a lunch. I don't know what this mentality is in dentistry that we all ... I see offices that have a no-show from 11-12, get an emergency call or walk-in 11:30, and they say, "We can't see you now because we're going to lunch at 12." It's like, what is going on? I'd rather work through lunch and then figure, well, maybe my 1 o'clock don't show. Being a fat boy, I could stand to miss a meal because these are future meals already eaten.

Colin: Bird in hands. It's better a bird in the bush.

Howard: Absolutely. A lot of it's ... The CEO is the culture. The mafia say that the fish rots from the head down. When I see all these attitudes, cultures, customs, beliefs of an office or a business, it starts with the doctor. If the doctor is the last one to work and the first one to go to lunch and the last one to come back from lunch and the first one to leave before 5, no one cares. When that doctor is the first one in there and that doctor says at the morning huddle, 'Yeah, I'll go through lunch." Look at an emergency room, treat other people like you want to be treated. When you go to an emergency room, you don't want to walk in the emergency room where everyone says, "It's dinnertime. We're all leaving." You just get her done.

Colin: How much of your time do you spend administratively or doing marketing in the practice?

Howard: Everybody has a different management style. You've got to do what you like and enjoy. My management style has always been find the very best people and get out of their way. I look at my business as the same as an NFL football team because the NFL player roster is 50. I got 50 employees. I own the football team, but I got a head coach. I've got an office manager. During the middle of the game, you don't see the owner calling the head coach and telling him plays. You don't see the owner getting involved with recruitment saying, "Get this wide receiver." You've got to find a coach. You've got to find an office manager. You've got to give him authority and responsibility to do their job.

You can't go around them. You can't have an office manager tell your four assistants, "This is how it's going to be," and then your assistants have been with you 15-28 years come whining to you and say, "Yeah, that's not right. I'm going to go tell the office manager no." I let them vent. Then I say, "Did you tell the office manager? What happened there?"

I see business as an orchestra. I have my back to the customers. I have my little deals. I'm not going to learn how to play the piano, I'm going to hire someone who plays the piano. I'm not going to learn how to play a tuba. I'm going to hire someone who plays the tuba. Look at Steve Thorn. He didn't even go to dental school and he owns 500 offices. He thought, "Hell, it's a lot easier to hire a dentist than to go to dental school." Steve Thorn ought to be a poster child to the fact that the people who have the biggest, most profitable offices in the world, they're not even dentists. They don't even do dentistry.

Get an office manager. Get out of their way. When you spend all of your time doing an MOD composite and you spend no time on tracking incoming calls, tracking marketing, making sure ... Someone doesn't come to their appointment. So many dentists say, "Wow, it's a no-show. I can't believe that idiot. They just made the appointment yesterday." Well, why don't you reach out? What if they were in a car wreck? What if their dog died? What if something happened?

Colin: Life happens.

Howard: Life happens. Life is filled with chaos. Focusing on ... I focus on ... I believe the key to any service business ... The key to the iPhone is the product. This iPhone is an amazing product. I don't know a single face behind this product, but we're in a service. A service is all about relations. It's about keeping the best long-term-relationship employees, and they'll hold long-term relationships with your customers. I like to focus on a lot of the stuff you do, like what is the new patient experience? When they call, do we answer it before two or three rings? Do we have five minutes to spend? Is it goes to voicemail or, "Can you please hold?"

When someone doesn't show, do we touch them back? If you think math and chemistry and geometry is complex, my God, meet a human. Humans are the most complex thing that I've ever even thought of. Your patient charge is ... It looks like a bar scene in *Star Wars*. They're just freaks of all natures. Some people, their fuse is this long and some people don't talk. Some will chat. Getting the people skills is always going to win, not the dental skills. It's going to always be the people skills. How you manage those new patient experience, you give them a tour of the office. When they walk in, do you stand up and say, "Hey." Call them by name.

Colin: Wow them.

Howard: Yeah.

Colin: What have you found to give you the best return in the marketing world? Internal marketing, external marketing? Where's your best return been for time or money spent?

Howard: I would say it's always going to be internal marketing. Again, it's a relationship business. We sell invisible. Nobody knows ... When I take my car into Lexus, I don't know if I need an oil change or the transmission fluid changed. They tell me this and that. You just got to look at them and say, "I trust the brand. You're in a uniform. You have a name tag. This dealership has been here for 25 years." It's all trust.

I think by keeping long-term staff, you'll keep long-term patients. I would rather ask a patient when I'm done working on you, say, "Hey, John, I haven't had any dentistry done in 25 years because I brush and floss every morning. I brush and floss every night. I get my teeth cleaned every three to six months."

I'm done working on you. If you do what the hygienists say and you do what they do, I'll never see you again. Do you personally know anybody who might need a dentist like me? If I gave you some cards, do you know anybody?

Hell, nine times out of 10 a human will say, "You know what, my buddy Joe at work, we just got dental insurance at work. My buddy Joe asked me who my dentist was. I'll send Joe down here." I think dentists don't ask for that because it takes humility. When the public describes physicians, dentists, and lawyers, the word "humility" does not make the top 100.

Colin: No. We do a lot of video shoots and shooting patient testimonials for docs. Every doctor we talk to says, "I don't know any patients that are going to come in. I don't know how I'm going to fill my schedule up with patients." I don't know that we've ever had an empty schedule. Patients are so willing to recommend and help. Alls you got to do is ask. Humility, just ask. Have a little bit of human contact. Everybody's very happy to recommend when they have a good experience.

Howard: It's also found to be biologically a hardwire. There's a book written by one of my MBA teachers at ASU called *The Reciprocal Factor ... The Reciprocity* – what was the name of that book? Basically, we're pack animals. Dogs, cats, monkeys, apes, humans. There's a science that when you say ... when I give you a gift, as a social animal, you're hardwired to want to return the gift.

That's why so many businesspeople want to take you to lunch because what they're playing on is a biological deal, where if I take you to lunch and you say, "Hey, I want to be your Farmer's Insurance agent and ensure your car," you just feel as a social pack animal that I should return the favor. You're hardwired to return the favor. When you actually ask a human, "By the way, do you know anybody you could refer to my practice?" They're hardwired biological at birth –

Colin: Are you familiar with Cialdini? Robert Cialdini?

Howard: Yeah, yeah, that's the guy.

Colin: That's who you're talking about?

Howard: What's the name of that book?

Colin: *Influence*.

Howard: *Influence*.

Colin: Fantastic book.

Howard: He was my teacher at MBA school.

Colin: Really?

Howard: Yeah, I live in Phoenix and he teaches at ASU. That's where I got my MBA in '98-99.

Colin: Wow, that's incredible.

Howard: He's an amazing guy. That's in like fifth edition. It's hardcore science. Another thing he talked about that they discovered is you always see ... now that I'm a grandpa, I see how my 25-year-old's talking to my 3-year-old. It's silly that I had to go to school eight years to be a dentist, but there's no training to be a parent. Humans routinely talk to babies in a 5, 10, 20,000-word vocabulary, and this baby doesn't even know 20, 30 words. One of the first things a baby human learns is that the minute you say "because," they know they're going to have to do it.

They say, "I want this." "No, because ..." and then all the – everything else is wa-wa-wa like on Lucy and Charlie because they don't know any of those words. He was the first guy that could measure that. When you say, "You need to get a root canal because ..." the minute you said "because," it flipped a switch unconsciously, and they already know they have to do the root canal.

Asking for influence, asking for reciprocity, using the word "because" – it's the most powerful word in humans.

Colin: Very cool. Very interesting. I've never heard that.

Howard: Of course now no one would say "because," because now that we're texters, it'd just be "cuz."

Colin: "Bc."

Howard: Yeah, "bc" or "cuz."

Colin: What's something that people might not know about you that you'd share with the viewers today?

Howard: That I'm actually tall, dark, and handsome. Almost everyone does not know that about me, but it's actually true. What did you say? What is something that people don't know about me?

Colin: The comedy club.

Howard: The comedy club, that might be fun. I think the comedy club is also an interesting perspective on life because life's tough. A lot of dentists will tell me a story like ... I've seen dentists where their practices burned out because they lost a 6-year-old to leukemia or they went through a divorce or this or that. Sometimes people will just tell you this hard story. They want an answer. The answer is, life's tough. It's tough. No one gets out alive. I like that Kansas atmosphere. In Kansas, it was amazing. Those are some of the toughest people.

There was a tornado. I grew up there, and a tornado would come through a farm town and literally erase a town of 5,000. Eight o'clock the next morning, what do they all do?

Colin: Did you hear about in Indiana, the tornado a couple of years ago that wiped out a whole high school? That was two miles from my office. It was devastating. They sent ... It was prom season, had a big prom dress drive because all those kids in high school had no prom dresses, nowhere to hold a prom. It was just –

Howard: What do they do?

Colin: Then they pull together.

Howard: And they just rebuild it.

Colin: They rebuild it.

Howard: You don't sit there and say, "We tried to have a school, then the tornado took it out." Life's tough. People are tough. That's another thing. I would really try to coach a staff on. A lot of times, a staff – the first impression of this patient coming in and this new patient coming in. You're seeing a not good side of them. I always remind my team, "We have no idea what they're going through. He could have just got off the phone and lost his grandpa. You don't know, or his dad."

You have no idea. Always give everybody a break. That's why I like comedy. Life's an attitude. When someone just comes in there and just being a horrible person, I just envision them as a 1-year-old baby and they're crying because they need changed, they're hungry, they're sleepy, someone stole their toy. We're all just big babies. You don't know what anybody's going through. Just cut them a lot of slack. Give them a lot of love and a lot of smiles. You'll build a successful practice.

Colin: Killer. Great advice. I really appreciate you being on the show today.

Howard: Thank you.

Colin: Thank you.

It's not a question of WHETHER you'll face the enormous forces described in this book.

It's only a question of WHEN.

You MUST prepare your practice, or risk losing everything you've worked so hard to build.

For a blueprint on how to defeat The Four Horsemen of Dentistry, call 888.741.1413 or go to www.DefeatThe4Horsemen.com